GW00319937

STEP-BY-STEP GARDEN GUIDES

Karlheinz Jacobi

Shrubs

Grange BOOKS

Step-by-Step Garden Guides
Ornamental Shrubs

Karlheinz Jacobi

German-language edition and photographs
Gärtnern leicht und richtig
Ziergehölze
© 1994 BLV Verlagsgesellschaft mbH, München

Translation:
Andrew Shackleton
Editing:
Asgard Publishing Services, Leeds
Typesetting:
Organ Graphic, Abingdon

English-language edition © 1995
Transedition Books, a division of
Andromeda Oxford Limited,
11-13 The Vineyard, Abingdon,
Oxfordshire OX14 3PX

This edition published in the UK in 1995 by Grange Books, an imprint of **Grange Books plc**, The Grange, Grange Yard, London SE1 3AG

Printed in 1995 in Dubai

ISBN 1 85627 718 6

Photographic credits
Apel 9 right, 42, 66; Bender 20, 27, 41, 43 top; CMA 46, 60/61, 76/77, 78, 79; Felbinger 2/3, 7, 8 bottom, 11, 12, 17, 18 right, 19, 22/23, 24/25, 30/31, 31, 32, 34/35, 43 bottom, 49, 50, 53, 54, 59, 62/63, 73, 74, 80/81, 82, 83, 84/85, 93; Gardena 75; Jacobi 18 left; Laux 33, 35, 37; Morell 8 top, 24, 26, 44, 45, 57, 89; Photos Horticultural 72, 92; Reinhard 9 left, 28/29, 40, 47, 48/49, 54/55, 56, 64, 65, 67, 68, 68/69, 86/87, 90; Sammer 6/7, 14, 70/71, 95; Seidl 13, 21, 38/39; Stehling 4/5, 10/11, 15, 16, 36, 51, 52, 58

CONTENTS

Ornamental shrubs — a world of choice

Trees and shrubs give shape to a garden. A garden without a tree is like a house without a roof. A tree can often provide a focal point for the rest of the garden. To achieve this it should normally stand alone, without being hemmed in by other large shrubs or bushes. You should also be able to see the trunk, the most visible expression of its strength and power.

Ornamental shrubs, on the other hand, have a variety of roles to play. Some evergreen or deciduous forms can be planted as hedges to mark the boundaries or sections of a garden. These hedges can be carefully trimmed or allowed to grow more freely. Some shrubs produce berries or thorns that can provide food or protection for birds. Others are a magnet for bees and butterflies. Many low-growing shrubs provide ground cover: they can prevent the soil from drying out, and stop unwanted weeds taking over. More specialised plants can be used in rock or heather gardens, or grown in tubs and troughs.

Far too few people realise that there are many shrubs — evergreens, especially — that flourish in the shade. Rhododendrons, for example, will flower beautifully in shady locations. Gardens have a tendency to become overcrowded, so that sun-loving plants are eventually starved of light. This is one reason why we've included a special section on shade-loving shrubs.

Flowering shrubs, especially those with a long flowering season, are another category we've highlighted. A long-lasting summer display is one of the things gardeners have come to expect. If the flowers are attractively scented, too, then that's an added bonus.

You also need to know which plants grow quickly, and which will flower only if males and females are planted together. Coniferous shrubs, including columnar varieties and those that will grow in tubs or troughs, form another major category.

Finally there's a wide choice of climbing shrubs that can be trained along frames, poles and pergolas, or used to create the vertical equivalent of a flowerbed on the walls of a house or garden.

This well-designed shrubbery provides an attractive frame for the garden beyond.

Trees and large shrubs with attractive flowers

A flowering tree provides the natural focus for a garden, and should be planted accordingly. It should stand completely on its own, well away from any other large, woody plants.

Indian bean tree
Catalpa bignonioides
A 33–50-ft (10–15-m) high tree with attractive flower clusters and interesting fruit, suitable only for large gardens. If your space is limited, look for the much smaller *C. b.* 'Nana' (stocked, but not always listed, by specialist nurseries).

Flowers: June–July, numerous white flower clusters.

Fruit: from September, brown pods 16 in (40 cm) long.

Position: sunny, but won't tolerate dryness.

Care: prune lightly, preferably only where damaged by frost.

Hawthorn
Crataegus
Gardeners argue a lot about planting hawthorn species in gardens. On the plus side, they are greatly valued for their delightful flowers and colourful fruits, which provide food for birds. As hedges they offer protection from intruders, and shelter for useful animals like shrews and hedgehogs. On the minus side, their branches are a breeding ground for pests at various stages of development. Hawthorns are also particularly vulnerable to fireblight, which means that some form of pest control is unavoidable.

If you still want to plant hawthorns, we recommend the following species and varieties:

C. 'Carrierei' grows to 16–23 ft (5–7 m), with long thorns, whitish-pink flowers and large, light red fruits.

C. coccinea grows to 16–23 ft (5–7 m), producing whitish to pink umbels in May, and striking dark red fruits later in the season.

C. persimilis 'Prunifolia' grows to 20–23 ft (6–7 m), with white umbels and numerous dark red fruits.

Position: sun to semi-shade.

Care: prune as necessary; can be renovated by pruning; never cut to a spherical shape.

Golden chain, common laburnum
Laburnum anagyroides
A small tree growing to 16 ft (5 m).

*The golden chain tree (*Laburnum anagyroides*) looks particularly good on its own.*

Flowers: May–June, yellow flowers hanging in long clusters (in *L. × watereri* 'Vossii' twice the size and even yellower), attractive to butterflies; seeds poisonous, so remove immediately.

Position: full sun to semi-shade.

Care: pruning unnecessary; will not tolerate renovation by pruning.

Magnolia
Magnolia

Among the most attractive of all flowering trees, but best in a garden when standing alone. The forms mentioned here grow to a maximum of 16 ft (5 m).

Chinese magnolia *(M. × soulangeana)* grows to 16 ft (5 m), and must have extra space in a garden. Flowers in April before the leaf shoots appear; blooms pink, upright and tulip-shaped, rather like upturned bells.

M. liliiflora **'Nigra':** 10–13 ft (3–4 m) high, upright and slow-growing. Flowers in April, but later than Chinese magnolia; blooms are dark red, but pink inside.

Position: sunny or well lit.

Care: avoid pruning if possible, though will tolerate drastic pruning.

The star magnolia (Magnolia stellata) deserves to be planted more often.

The lovely blooms of the Chinese magnolia

Crab apple
Malus

Ornamental crab apples produce gorgeous blossoms from May to June, followed by decorative fruits in the autumn. The flowers are single or double, varying in colour from white through pink to scarlet, wine-red or purple. Varieties are available as standards (13–33 ft; 4–10 m) or as bushes, which are strongly recommended.

Position: full sun to well lit.

Care: thin out by pruning at the end of the winter.

Recommended species and varieties: *M.* 'Charlottae': flowers in late May, soft pink, violet fragrance; fruit greenish-yellow; available as bush. *M.* 'Eleyi': flowers May, dark purple; fruits a similar colour; available as bush. *M. floribunda*: flowers in May, soft pink; fruits plentiful and long-lasting, yellow, turning red in the sun; available as bush or standard. *M.* 'Hillieri': flowers profusely in late May, light pink, semi-double; long-lasting fruit, yellowish-orange; available as bush. *M.* 'Profusion': flowers profusely in late May, wine-red, fading later; fruit carmine red; available as bush. *M.* 'Prof.

Sprenger': flowers in May, soft pink, then white; long-lasting orange fruit; bush or standard. *M.* 'Royalty': flowers in late May, carmine red; fruit dark red; bush or standard.

Foxglove tree
Paulownia tomentosa

A medium-sized tree, with older plants growing to 33–50 ft (10–15 m). Needs a solitary position in a large garden.

Flowers: May, light blue bell-shaped flowers in upright clusters 12 in (30 cm) high.

Position: sun to semi-shade, lime-loving.

Care: young plants tolerate pruning, older plants are more vulnerable.

Prunus 'Amanogawa' is a columnar cherry that will fit in even the smallest garden.

The dwarf Russian almond (Prunus tenella) always stays small and pretty.

The lovely pink blossoms of this flowering cherry create an unforgettable display.

Ornamental cherries
Prunus species and varieties
Flowering trees and shrubs with various growth habits, noted for their rich displays of blossom.

Flowers: season varies from March to June depending on the variety ('Autumnalis' flowers from late autumn to April); colour white with mainly pink (but sometimes red) tints.

Position: sunny or well lit, likes a deep, porous soil.

Care: avoid pruning in case the sap runs, but saw off sick or overgrown branches immediately, before the leaves are shed.

Recommended species and varieties: 'Accolade': 10-13 ft (3-4 m); pink, slightly double flowers in April. 'Amanogawa': columnar habit, 13-16 ft (4-5 m); light pink, slightly double flowers April-May. *P. subhirtella* 'Autumnalis': spreading habit, 13-16 ft (4-5 m); conspicuous white to pale pink semi-double flowers from late autumn until April. 'Fukubana': broad habit, 13-20 ft (4-6 m); dark pink (later light pink) flowers in April. 'Kanzan': small tree or large shrub, 23-33 ft (7-10 m); dark pink, densely double flowers in April (particularly beautiful). 'Kiku-shidare Zakura': small tree with branches drooping to the ground, 10-16 ft (3-5 m); pink, densely double flowers April-May.

Cherry plum
Prunus cerasifera 'Nigra'
A small tree growing to 16 ft (5 m), with overhanging branches and deep purple leaves. The pink flowers appear in April, and the fruits are edible.

Position: sun to semi-shade.

Care: pruning possible but not necessary.

Dwarf Russian almond
Prunus tenella
A broad, bushy shrub growing to 30-40 in (80-100 cm).

Flowers: April-May, red single flowers growing densely on shoots from the previous year.

Position: sunny and bright, likes humous, lime-rich soils.

Care: prune back the flower shoots at once after flowering.

Dwarf almond
Prunus triloba
A beautiful spring-flowering shrub. Can be grown as a standard.

Flowers: late April, pink, densely double flowers.

Position: sunny and bright, lime-loving, plant as solitary.

Care: prune back the flower shoots straight after flowering.

Shrubs with a long flowering season

Most of these long-flowering shrubs flower in the summer or autumn; *Viburnum* × *bodnantense* 'Dawn', for instance, doesn't come into flower until late in the autumn.

Butterfly bush
Buddleia davidii hybrids
So called because of their popularity with butterflies seeking nectar, these shrubs with their beautiful flowers are suitable for any garden. Different varieties grow to 7–10 ft (2–3 m), offering a choice of flower colours.

Flowers: between July and October depending on the variety; sweet-smelling.

Position: sunny or dappled shade.

Care: shorten the soft shoot tips in the autumn, and in spring cut back the flowered shoots from the previous year.

Buddleia alternifolia
Grows to 10 ft (3 m) with gently drooping branches. Beautiful, but needs plenty of space.

Flowers: June, lilac-purple.

Position: sun to semi-shade.

Care: no pruning.

*A butterfly bush (*Buddleia davidii hybrid*)*

Ling, heather
Calluna vulgaris cultivars
The most interesting varieties of this summer-flowering heather are those that grow to between

8 in (20 cm) and 2 ft (60 cm), and flower in August and September. In the case of 'Annemarie', 'H. E. Beale' and 'Peter Sparkes', the flowers don't

appear until September or October. 'Aurea' has yellow leaves that turn bronze-coloured in winter, while 'Gold Haze' has yellow leaves all year round.

Position: sun to semi-shade, no lime.

Care: prune back gently every other year, after flowering or in spring before growth starts.

Caryopteris
Caryopteris clandonensis **'Heavenly Blue'**
A dwarf shrub growing to 24–31 in (60-80 cm), with loosely growing upright shoots.

Flowers: August–October, blue, in long clusters (valuable summer-flowering shrub).

Position: full sun or well lit.

Care: prune as necessary in spring; flowers appear in the same year after pruning.

Californian lilac
Ceanothus hybrids
A valuable flowering shrub that grows up to 15 ft (4.5 m), depending on variety.

Flowers: May–October or until first frosts, in long or rounded clusters, mainly shades of blue.

Position: full sun or well lit.

Care: prune spring or autumn, depending on flowering time.

Heath
Erica carnea hybrids
Evergreen ground-cover sub-shrubs, generally no higher than 8 in (20 cm).

Heathers (Calluna) for flowerbeds and plant pots

Varieties: 'Alba': white flowers, January–April, 10 in (25 cm). 'Atrorubra': carmine red, March–May, 8 in (20 cm). 'Myretoun Ruby': bright red, March–May, 6 in (15 cm). 'Snow Queen': pure white, January–April, 8 in (20 cm). 'Vivellii': violet-red, Mar– Apr, 8 in (20 cm). 'Winter Beauty': pink, December–March, 6-8 in (15-20 cm).

Position: sunny or well lit, lime-tolerating.

Care: prune lightly after flowering.

Cornish heath
Erica vagans 'Mrs D. F. Maxwell'
Grows higher than *E. carnea* (12-20 in; 30-50 cm), evergreen.

Flowers: July–September, cherry-pink.

Position: sunny or well lit.

*Witch hazel (*Hamamelis*) will flower even in ice and snow.*

Shrubby hibiscus
Hibiscus syriacus hybrids
A valuable shrub that grows very upright to a height of 5–7 ft (1.5–2 m).

Flowers: late July to first frosts, single or double, although double varieties need plenty of sun and warmth. Varieties include 'Coelestis' (violet-blue), 'Hamabo' (soft pink with reddish streaks), 'Pink Giant' (pure pink), 'Red Heart' (white with red centre), 'William R. Smith' (pure white) and 'Woodbridge' (deep red with darker centre).

Position: full sun to well lit, but doesn't like dry conditions; protect from frost.

Care: prune back previous year's shoots regularly, before new growth starts.

Winter jasmine
Jasminum nudiflorum
A 7-ft (2-m) high scrambling climber with slender green shoots that should be tied to a trellis. Will also hang down from the top of a wall, or can be planted between leafless shrubs that will provide anchorage.

Flowers: yellow, like primulas; often appear first in November, thereafter until March.

Position: lime-loving, undemanding, tolerates poor soils.

Care: thin out if branches become overcrowded; tolerates drastic pruning.

Care: prune lightly after flowering.

Witch hazel
Hamamelis hybrids
A group of pretty winter-flowering shrubs, all noted for their lovely autumn colouring. The large-flowered hybrids are particularly suitable for gardens. Among the nicest varieties are 'Diane' (red or light red), 'Feuerzauber' (bronze-red), 'Jelena' (bright orange, Dec), 'Pallida' (light yellow, Dec), and 'Ruby Glow' (light red). The hybrids reach 10 ft (3 m) in height; they grow slowly, often producing bizarre shapes.

Japanese witch hazel (*H. japonica*) has small yellow flowers (December–March).

Chinese witch hazel (*H. mollis*) grows to only 7 ft (2 m) and has large golden flowers (December–March).

Position: sunny or well lit.

Care: renovation pruning OK.

Perovskia atriplicifolia
A greyish-leaved sub-shrub growing to about 4 ft (1.2 m), noted for late flowering season.

Flowers: blue spikes from August onwards.

Position: sunny and bright; thrives on any soil; often dies back to the ground with frost, but grows again afterwards.

Care: if it hasn't died back, prune back to ground level after winter.

Shrubby cinquefoil
Potentilla fruticosa varieties
This small bushy shrub grows to between 16 in (40 cm) and 5 ft (1.5 m), depending on variety.

Flowers: May–Oct non-stop; flowers at once after planting.

Position: sun to semi-shade; robust but sensitive to heat and dryness.

Care: prune and thin regularly to encourage maximum flowering.

Recommended varieties:
'Arbuscula': light yellow flowers, Jun–Sep, 24–31 in (60–80 cm) tall. 'Farreri': dark yellow, Jun–Sep, 24–39 in (60–100 cm). 'Goldfinger': lemon yellow, Jun–Aug, 3–7 ft (1–2 m). 'Hachmanns Gigant': golden yellow, Jun–Sep, 20–28 in (50–70 cm). 'Klondike': light yellow, Jun–Aug, 39–47 in (100–120 cm). 'Red Ace': reddish inside, yellow outside, Jun–Jul, 16–24 in (40–60 cm).

Weigelas grow up to 10 ft (3 m) high, and are simply covered with flowers.

Winter-flowering cherry
Prunus subhirtella
'Autumnalis'
A pretty tree with slender shoots, growing to 13–16 ft (4–5 m). The leaves turn a lovely yellowy-orange in autumn.

Flowers: late autumn to March; white, semi-double, conspicuous.

Position: sun to semi-shade; avoid stagnant, wet soil.

Care: avoid pruning if possible, but saw off sick or dried-out branches just before leaf drop.

Winter viburnum
Viburnum × bodnantense
'Dawn'
Grows to 7 ft (2 m) with a loose, upright habit.

Flowers: October–March; deep pink, becoming paler, fragrant.

Position: well lit; also semi-shade or shade.

Care: avoid pruning if possible.

Weigela
Weigela hybrids
These broad, bushy shrubs grow to 3–10 ft (1–3 m). Hybrid weigelas have the best flowers.

Varieties: 'Bristol Ruby': carmine red flowers, May–June; 'Eva Rathke': carmine red, June–August; 'Newport Red': deep red, June–July; 'Styriaca': carmine red, May–June.

Position: sun to semi-shade.

Care: thin out every 2–3 years.

13

Shrubs with fragrant blossom

Some shrubs — roses, or mock orange, for example — are well known for their scent. Many others manage to keep their lovely scents a well-guarded secret, often because you need to bend down to the flowers if you want to smell them. Some flowers broadcast their scent; others retain it, so you must hold them close to your face to discover it.

Butterfly bush
Buddleia davidii hybrids
This 7–10-ft (2–3-m) tall shrub gets its name from the hosts of butterflies it attracts. There are many varieties with lovely flowers in assorted colours.

Flowers: between July and October, depending on the variety; fragrant.

Position: sunny to well lit.

Care: shorten the soft shoot tips in the autumn; in spring cut back the flowered shoots from the previous year.

Carolina allspice
Calycanthus floridus
A 7-ft (2-m) high bushy shrub with bark that smells like cloves.

Flowers: June–July, large, dark red, highly fragrant but hidden behind leaves.

Position: full sun to semi-shade.

Care: thin out only very gradually.

Winter hazel
Corylopsis pauciflora
A highly decorative spring-flowering shrub that grows to 6 ft (1.8 m).

Flowers: March–April, yellow, spreading in clusters all over the plant.

Position: semi-shade to shade.

Care: strictly no pruning!

*The fragrant blooms of the butterfly bush (*Buddleia davidii*) are a magnet for butterflies.*

Broom

Cytisus and *Chamaecytisus*
These shrubs are suitable for
rock gardens, heather gardens,
borders and sunny positions. In
spring the air is filled with the
scent of their flowers. Species
and hybrids include both low-
growing and taller forms that
make the garden look quite
distinctive in spring.

Low-growing brooms

Cytisus ×*beanii*: 12 in (30
cm) high, 31 in (80 cm) wide;
deep yellow flowers in May.

C. decumbens: 8 in (20 cm)
high, 24 in (60 cm) wide,
ground cover; yellow flowers
May–July.

C. ×*kewensis*: 12-20 in (30-50
cm) high, broad habit; creamy
flowers from May onwards.

Purple broom (*Chamaecytisus purpureus*): 16-24 in (40-60
cm) high, up to 31 in (80 cm)
wide; purple to pink flowers
June–July.

Taller-growing brooms

Common broom (*Cytisus
scoparius*): 3-7 ft (1-2 m) tall,
broad habit; bright yellow
flowers, highly fragrant, May–
June.

Cultivated brooms (*Cytisus*
hybrids): 3-7 ft (1-2 m) tall, with
a dense, bushy habit and drooping, loosely growing or upright
shoots depending on the variety.
The flowering season varies
according to variety, with a
glorious riot of colours.

*If you like strong scents,
try some of the many
cultivated brooms
(Cytisus hybrids).*

**Recommended
varieties:** 'Allgold': golden
yellow, early-flowering; 'Hollan-
dia': purple and yellow, early;
'Burkwoodii': carmine red, late;
'Dragonfly': yellow with red,
early; 'Luna': light and dark
yellow, late; 'Roter Favorit': red,
late; other varieties similar in
colour and habit.

Position: sunny or well-lit.

15

Purple broom (Chamaecytisus purpureus) grows to only 20 in (50 cm).

Care: Water well after planting. In the case of taller-growing brooms, cut back part of the new shoots every year after flowering. Low-growing forms won't need any pruning.

Mezereon
Daphne mezereum

This small, 3-ft (1-m) high shrub is beautiful but poisonous. It comes into flower unusually early, which makes it popular with bees.

Flowers: February–March before the leaves appear, red–purple, highly fragrant. *D. m.* 'Alba' has white flowers in May. *D. m.* 'Somerset' bears fragrant pale pink flowers in May–June.

Fruits: the red fruits of species and *D. m.* 'Alba' are extremely poisonous, and must be removed if children could pick them; otherwise choose *D. m.* 'Somerset', which has no fruits.

Position: sun to semi-shade.

Care: don't prune, or it won't flower.

Garland flower
Daphne cneorum

A dwarf shrub growing to 8–20 in (20–50 cm).

Flowers: April–May, carmine red, sweet fragrance, beautiful.

Position: sunny or well lit.

Care: don't feed or prune.

Witch hazel
Hamamelis hybrids

A pretty, winter-flowering shrub noted for its lovely autumn colouring. The large-flowered hybrids are best. The hybrids grow slowly up to about 10 ft

(3 m), and are often bizarrely shaped. **Japanese witch hazel** (*H. japonica*) has small yellow flowers from December to March. **Chinese witch hazel** (*H. mollis*) grows to only 7 ft (2 m) and has large golden flowers (also December–March).

Position: sunny or well lit.

Care: don't prune.

Golden chain, common laburnum
Laburnum anagyroides
A small tree growing to 16 ft (5 m).

Flowers: May–June, yellow flowers hanging in long clusters (twice the size and even yellower in *L. × watereri* 'Vossii'), attractive to butterflies.

Fruits: the seeds are poisonous, so must be removed immediately.

Position: full sun to semi-shade.

Care: doesn't need pruning, and won't tolerate drastic pruning.

Goatleaf honeysuckle
Lonicera caprifolium
A climbing shrub that grows vigorously to 10–16 ft (3–5 m).

Flowers: May–June, a profusion of yellowish-white flowers, reddish outside.

Fruits: coral-red berries, highly poisonous.

Warminster broom (Cytisus × praecox) fills the whole garden with its scent.

Position: damp, lime-rich soil in a shaded location.

Care: renovation pruning recommended.

Gold flame honeysuckle
L. × heckrottii
A lovely twining shrub growing to 10–13 ft (3–4 m).

Flowers: from June through to autumn, a profusion of red flowers, later yellow and red.

Fruits: poisonous berries.

Position/care: as for goatleaf honeysuckle.

Magnolia
Magnolia
A group of valuable flowering trees of varying heights. Their beauty can be fully appreciated only if they are standing alone.

Chinese magnolia
Magnolia × soulangeana
Grows to 16 ft (5 m).

Flowers: April, before leaves appear, pink, upright like tulips.

Position: sunny or well lit.

Care: don't prune if possible, though it can tolerate drastic pruning.

Left Mahonia bealei *deserves more attention than it gets.*

Right Philadelphus *are undemanding shrubs, yet have beautifully fragrant flowers.*

Oregon grape
Mahonia aquifolium
A small evergreen bush that reaches 7 ft (2 m) at the most, with spiny-edged leaves that turn purple in winter.

Flowers: April, yellow, highly fragrant.

Fruits: pretty, round blue berries from July onwards.

Position: sun to shade, very robust.

Care: renovation pruning recommended.

Mahonia bealei
This extremely valuable and upright-growing shrub has long, spiny-edged evergreen leaves and grows to heights of 3-5 ft (1-1.5 m).

Flowers: February–April (can be earlier), yellow, fragrant.

Fruits: conspicuous dark blue berries from July into the autumn.

Position: sun to shade.

Care: pruning possible, but best avoided on account of the growth habit.

Crab apple
Malus
Crab apples provide magnificent blossoms May–June, followed by decorative fruits in autumn. The flowers are single or double, varying in colour from white through pink to scarlet, wine-red or purple. Those of the 'Charlottae' variety (available as a bush) are especially fragrant; its pink blossoms appear at the end of May, and the fruits are yellow. Varieties come either as standards (13-33 ft; 4-10 m) or bushes, better for gardens.

Position: full sun to well lit.

Care: thin out by pruning at the end of the winter.

Tree peony
Paeonia suffruticosa

An upright shrub growing to 3 ft (1 m), with a glorious display of flowers.

Flowers: May, white, yellow, pink, red and shades in between, semi-double to double.

Position: needs a nutritious soil with plenty of humus, and a warm, sunny location; winter protection required.

Care: plant deep enough to put the graft union below soil level; don't use peat, and don't prune.

Philadelphus

A group of beautiful but un-demanding shrubs that grow to 3-10 ft (1-3 m) depending on species or variety.

Flowers: May–July, white, sweet-smelling; single, semi-double or double.

Position: sun to shade, but with fewer flowers in the shade; undemanding.

Care: feed regularly in the spring; prune after flowering, thinning out older plants; drastic pruning possible.

Mock orange, syringa (*P. coronarius*): grows to 10 ft (3 m), single flowers, ideal for hedges.

Recommended varieties: 'Rosace': magnificent semi-double flowers; 'Erectus': single flowers, 5-7 ft (1.5-2 m); 'Girandole': double flowers (even on young plants), 3-5 ft (1-1.5 m); *P. coronarius* 'Variegatus': leaves edged with cream, single flowers, up to 13 ft (4 m); 'Boule d'Argent': dense clusters of large double flowers, 7 ft (2 m).

Andromeda
Pieris

P. floribunda: grows to 3 ft (1 m) and produces upright clusters of white flowers April–May. 'Forest Flame' is less vigorous than the species, with bright red young leaves and shoots.

Lily-of-the-valley bush (*P. japonica*): grows to 7-10 ft (2-3 m), with hanging clusters of white flowers from March to May. 'Variegata' grows to 30-40 in (80-100 cm), and has leaves variegated creamy white.

Position: shade (except 'Forest Flame') to semi-shade, acid soil.

Care: no pruning and no inorganic fertilisers (use blood-fish-and-bone or bonemeal).

Common elder
Sambucus nigra

This 16-ft (5-m) high shrub provides food for birds.

Flowers: clusters of large, white, aromatic flowers.

Fruits: June–August; black berries can be made into wine or elderberry cordial.

The tree peony (Paeonia suffruticosa) produces some gorgeous flowers.

19

Position: sun to semi-shade; humus- and nutrient-rich soil.

Care: will tolerate even drastic pruning.

American elder
Sambucus canadensis
'Maxima'
Grows to 10-13 ft (3-4 m).

Flowers: like common elder, but flower heads very large.

Fruits: from August, edible purple–black berries.

Position/care: as for common elder.

Lilac
Syringa vulgaris cultivars
These shrubs come in various bush or standard forms, and in single or double varieties.

Flowers: May, fragrant.

Single-flowered varieties: 'Souvenir de Louis Späth', dark purple; 'Primrose', primrose yellow.

Double varieties: 'Charles Joly', purplish-red with lighter-coloured flower tips; 'Katharine Havemeyer', lilac to purplish-pink, densely semi-double; 'Michel Buchner', lilac with a white 'eye'; 'Madame Lemoine', pure white; 'Mrs Edward Harding', purplish-red to -pink.

Position: sunny or well lit, but never in shade or semi-shade; prefers a well-drained, humus-rich soil.

Care: thin out after flowering; cut out bare branches; tolerates renovation pruning.

Rouen lilac
Syringa × chinensis
Highly recommended for a roomy garden, this thick, bushy shrub grows to 7-10 ft (2-3 m) and has elegantly overhanging branches, with drooping clusters of lavender-coloured flowers.

Flowers: from May onwards, lilac-coloured flowers; the weaker-growing 'Saugeana' variety has darker, more purple-hued flowers.

Position: sunny, but no direct sunlight; sensitive to drought.

Care: if possible avoid pruning, though it will tolerate renovation; remove all dead flowers.

The valuable Rouen lilac (Syringa × chinensis) develops a thick, bushy habit.

Cultivated lilacs (Syringa) come in a variety of bushy and half-standard forms.

Viburnum
Viburnum species and varieties

This highly varied genus contains both evergreen and deciduous species that flower in the winter, spring or summer; all those included here have beautifully fragrant flowers.

Winter-flowering forms

V. × bodnantense 'Dawn': 7–8 ft (2–2.5 m), loosely upright habit; fragrant deep pink flowers (later turning paler) October–March.

V. farreri: 7–10 ft (2–3 m), loosely branching habit; fragrant white flowers, pink in bud, February–March (often as early as November).

Spring-flowering forms

V. × carlcephalum: 7 ft (2 m), broad bushy habit, suitable as a solitary or for ornamental hedges; large, pink-budded white clusters of fragrant flowers, April–May.

V. carlesii: 3 ft (1 m), broad bushy habit; strongly fragrant pink to white flowers ('Aurora' has darker flowers, red opening to pink) April–May.

Chinese wisteria
Wisteria sinensis

A vigorously climbing shrub with rope-like shoots that grow up to 33 ft (10 m) long. Looks especially good on a house wall or pergola, but needs the assistance of a climbing frame or plenty of wire. Note in particular that all parts of this plant are poisonous.

Flowers: April–May, 12-in (30-cm) long clusters of gently fragrant, light purple flowers.

Position: sunny, well sheltered.

Care: many wisterias may take some years to come into flower, but a plant that persistently refuses to flower may be a non-flowering seedling. If so, dig it up. It's important to prune back the side shoots from the current year. If possible, cut them back by half their length immediately after flowering, and down to one bud in winter.

Wisteria is particularly suitable for house walls and pergolas, but can also be trained up the trunk of a laburnum. The clusters of purple flowers make an attractive contrast with the yellow of the laburnum.

21

Shrubs with distinctively coloured leaves

Trees and shrubs with colourful leaves can provide a feast for the eyes that lasts for months on end, often from the first spring shoots to the last leaf of autumn. Many of these foliage plants are even more colourful than the flowering shrubs, though a garden probably looks best with a mixture of the two.

Whitish or partly white leaves

Box elder

Acer negundo cultivars
Tall, fast-growing shrubs with a loose habit, reaching 16–23 ft (5-7 m).

Varieties: 'Flamingo', light pink leaf margins at first, later with white variegations; 'Variegatum', leaves with white or variegated edges, preceded (March–April) by yellowish-white flowers.

Position: sun to semi-shade.

Care: no unnecessary pruning, but remove reversions (shoots with green leaves).

Red-barked dogwood

Cornus alba 'Elegantissima'
This 7-ft (2-m) high shrub has dark red bark and white-edged leaves; sunlight produces strong colouring in both bark and leaves.

Position: sun to semi-shade.

Care: no pruning if at all possible.

Euonymus fortunei

The 'Emerald Gaiety' variety is a creeping (8 in; 20 cm) or climbing (3 ft; 1 m) shrub with white-edged leaves. 'Variegatus' is similar, but has silvery leaf margins and climbs to 5 ft (1.5 m).

Position: sun to semi-shade.

Care: don't prune, just let it grow.

Andromeda

Pieris japonica 'Variegata'
About 30–40 in (80–100 cm) tall, with upright clusters of white flowers (April–May) and white-variegated leaves.

Position: well lit to semi-shaded; must have acid soil.

Care: no inorganic fertilisers (use blood-fish-and-bone or bonemeal); no pruning.

Yellowish or partly yellow leaves

Maple

Acer shirasawanum aureum
A 5-ft (1.5-m) high dwarf shrub, whose golden yellow leaf shoots develop into leaves tinged with greenish-yellow. Unsuitable for sunny locations.

Position: semi-shade, avoid direct sun at all costs.

Care: avoid pruning if at all possible.

Box elder

Acer negundo 'Aureo-variegatum'
Grows to 16–23 ft (5-7 m) and has yellow-variegated leaves.

Position: sun to semi-shade.

Care: try not to prune.

Ling, heather
Calluna vulgaris cultivars
The most interesting varieties of this summer-flowering heather grow to 8–24 in (20–60) cm and flower August–September. 'Aurea' has yellow leaves that turn bronze-coloured in winter, while those of 'Gold Haze' remain yellow all year round.

Position: sun to semi-shade; no lime.

Care: prune every other year.

Yellow-leaved dogwoods
Cornus varieties

Red-barked dogwood (*C. alba* 'Spaethii'): grows to 5 ft (1.5 m), with gold-edged (or completely yellow) leaves, and brownish-red or dark-red bark.

Yellow osier dogwood (*C. stolonifera* 'Flaviramea'): 7–10 ft (2–3 m) tall, with yellowish-green leaves and yellowish-green bark.

Position: sun to semi-shade.

Care: don't prune dogwoods if at all possible.

Euonymus fortunei
The 'Emerald and Gold' variety is a creeping (8 in; 20 cm) or climbing (5 ft; 1.5 m) shrub with yellow-and-green leaves.

Position: sun to semi-shade.

Care: don't prune, just let it grow.

English ivy
Hedera helix 'Oro di Bogliasco'
A good climber; its leaves are small and have central gold patches.

Position: sunny to shaded.

Care: prune as much as you like.

Yellow hollies
Ilex varieties
I. × altaclerensis 'Golden King' (female) has leaves with broad yellow margins, and grows to 7–10 ft (2–3 m). *I. aquifolium* 'Golden van Tol' (female) has similarly yellow leaf margins. The leaves are almost spineless.

This yellow-leaved box elder (Acer negundo 'Aureovariegatum') brightens up the garden all year round.

Position: sun to semi-shade.

Care: prune only after frost damage.

*A white-variegated lily-of-the-valley bush (*Pieris japonica *'Variegata')*

Yellow privet
Ligustrum ovalifolium 'Aureum'
Different from the green privet in having gold-edged or completely yellow leaves. Grows rather less vigorously than the species, reaching only 7–10 ft (2–3 m) in height.

Position: likes sun to semi-shade.

Care: prune as much as you like.

Golden elm
Ulmus minor 'Dampieri Aurea'
A 26-ft (8-m) tall tree with a slender, upright habit and wrinkled, golden yellow leaves. Must be planted as a solitary.

Position: sunny or well lit.

*A red form of the Japanese maple (*Acer palmatum atropurpureum*)*

Silvery-grey to silvery-blue leaves

Caryopteris
Caryopteris × clandonensis
'Heavenly Blue'
A dwarf shrub growing to 24–31 in (60–80 cm), with loosely growing upright shoots.

Flowers: August–October, blue, in long clusters (valuable summer-flowering shrub).

Position: full sun or well lit.

Care: prune as necessary in spring; flowers appear in the same year after pruning.

Sea buckthorn
Hippophae rhamnoides
A loose, bushy shrub with prickly branches that grows to 10–16 ft (3–5 m).

Fruits: conspicuous orange berries on the female forms, edible and high in vitamin C.

Position: full sun or dappled shade.

Care: more fruit if left unpruned, but will tolerate drastic pruning.

Perovskia atriplicifolia
A grey-leaved sub-shrub (4 ft; 1.2 m) noted for its late flowering period and its aromatic leaves.

Flowers: blue, from August onwards.

Position: sunny and bright; thrives on any soil; often dies back to the ground with frost, but grows again afterwards.

Care: if it hasn't died back, prune to the ground after the winter.

Silver-leaved creeping willow
Salix repens argentea
Grows to only 12-20 in (30-50 cm) and spreads over the ground, with yellow catkins in April.

Position: sunny or well lit.

Care: no pruning.

Reddish or purple leaves

Japanese maple
Acer palmatum
A. p. atropurpureum is a highly decorative shrub with a broad, bushy habit growing to

Sea buckthorn (Hippophae rhamnoides) has leaves that shine like silver.

10 ft (3 m). It bears purple leaves from spring through to autumn, with purple flowers at the beginning of July.

'Dissectum' grows to 3 ft (1 m) high and 7 ft (2 m) wide, with a spherical habit and deeply divided leaves. Leaf colour varies according to the sub-variety: 'Atropurpureum' blood-red; 'Garnet' orange-red; 'Nigrum' dark purple; 'Viridis' green.

Position: sun to semi-shade, though direct sunlight can burn the leaves; prefers cool, damp soil (plant around with weak-rooted perennials).

Care: avoid pruning if possible.

Barberry
Berberis subspecies and varieties

B. thunbergii atropurpurea grows to 3-5 ft (1-1.5 m), with reddish-brown leaves that turn bright red in the autumn.

B. ×ottawensis 'Superba' (formerly *B. t.* 'Atropurpurea Superba') grows to 10-13 ft (3-4 m), with a sturdy, umbrella-like habit and brownish-red leaves.

'Atropurpurea Nana', the dwarf form of *B. t. atropurpurea* (12-20 in; 30-50 cm), makes good boundary hedges.

Flowers: May, yellow-and-red.

Fruits: bright red; particularly attractive after the leaves have been shed.

Position: sun to semi-shade; likes all garden soils.

Care: tolerates pruning, even of the most drastic kind.

Purple filbert
Corylus maxima 'Purpurea'
Grows to 10-13 ft (3-4 m). Similar to the cobnut (*C. avellana*), but less vigorous, and with dark purple leaves.

Flowers: March–April, reddish catkins.

Fruits: edible brown nuts.

Position: sun to semi-shade.

Care: thinning recommended; plant several varieties to ensure pollination.

Smoke tree
Cotinus coggygria 'Royal Purple'
This beautiful and unusual variety grows to 7–10 ft (2–3 m), but is less vigorous than the green-leaved species.

Flowers: June–July, greenish-red, in long clusters.

Fruits: reddish, from late July.

Position: sunny or dappled shade.

Care: don't prune.

Crab apple
Malus
This popular ornamental has a number of red-leaved varieties. 'Eleyi': pink flowers mid-May; yellow/red fruit. 'Aldenhamensis': dark red flowers in May; red–purple fruit. 'Profusion': wine-red flowers end of May; red-brown fruit. 'Royalty': carmine red flowers end of May; dark red fruit.

Position: full sun or well lit.

Care: thin out branches after the winter.

Ornamental plums
Prunus hybrids and varieties

Cherry plum (*P. cerasifera* 'Nigra'): a small tree or large shrub growing to 16 ft (5 m), with drooping branches and purple leaves; goes well with white-flowered shrubs; pink blossoms from April onwards; delicious fruits.

P. × **cistena**: similar to the cherry plum but much smaller (7–8 ft; 2–2.5 m); white single flowers in May, and edible fruits in autumn.

P. × **blireana:** a small tree (16 ft; 5 m) with a thick, bushy habit (as wide as it is tall), slightly drooping branches and bronze-purple leaves (later green); pink, semi-double flowers (April–May).

Position: sun to semi-shade.

Care: pruning possible but not necessary.

*Everything is red about this smoke tree (*Cotinus coggygria *'Royal Purple'), from the bark to the leaves and the flowers.*

27

Shrubs that will fruit only if you put male and female plants together

The best example of this is the sea buckthorn (*Hippophae rhamnoides*). The female plants bear a massive harvest of berries rich in vitamin C, but won't produce anything unless there's at least one male plant close by to pollinate them. The same is true for other shrubs that produce decorative as opposed to edible fruits.

Broadleaves

Actinidia
Actinidia arguta
A broad, vigorously twining shrub with long stems that grow to 16 ft (5 m); beautiful autumn foliage. Support required.

Flowers: May–June, fragrant white umbels hidden in the foliage.

Fruits: edible berries high in vitamin C.

Position: sunny, warm.

Care: prune back only young shoots.

Staff vine
Celastrus orbiculatus
This vine will climb to 33 ft (10 m) on a pergola, but will tend to strangle a tree. Leaves turn yellow in autumn.

Fruits: yellow-and-scarlet, beautiful but poisonous.

Position: sun to shade.

Care: prune where necessary.

Sea buckthorn
Hippophae rhamnoides
A loose, bushy shrub with prickly branches and growing to 10-16 ft (3-5 m).

Fruits: conspicuous orange berries, edible and high in vitamin C.

Position: full sun or dappled shade.

Care: produces more fruit if left unpruned, but will tolerate drastic pruning.

Holly
Ilex varieties
This slow-growing shrubby tree (26-33 ft; 8-10 m) with its prickly leaves is the ideal haven for birds, producing a rich harvest of fruit. We particularly recommend the varieties with variegated leaves: 'Argentea Marginata', slow-growing with white-edged leaves; 'Golden King', with broad yellow leaf margins; and 'Golden van Tol', with similarly yellow leaf margins. All are female.

Prickly heath
Pernettya mucronata
This small shrub grows to only 3-5 ft (1-1.5 m), and makes a good companion plant for dwarf rhododendrons, heaths and heathers.

Fruits: large round berries, white, pink, red or purple, and very pretty.

Flowers: May–July, white to pink.

Position: well lit to shaded; acid soil.

Care: no pruning.

Stag's horn sumach
Rhus hirta
A large, many-stemmed shrub (13-16 ft; 4-5 m) with reddish-

brown velvety bark, and beautiful orange, yellow and red autumn colouring. The slower-growing *R. h.* 'Laciniata' has finely divided leaves and a more spreading habit.

Flowers/fruits: green male flowers (from July) and hairy crimson fruits are the main features of interest.

Position: sunny; light soil.

Care: no pruning if possible.

Skimmia
Skimmia japonica
Slow-growing, 24 in (60 cm) tall.

Flowers: April–May, white clusters, often fragrant.

Fruits: round red berries lasting into the winter.

Position: sun to shade.

Care: cut off only frost-damaged shoots.

Conifers

Chinese juniper
Juniperus chinensis
'Keteleeri'
Grows to 5-7 ft (1.5-2 m), taller after 15 years; loose columnar habit; many small, light green cones. Will grow on any soil in sun or shade.

Pencil cedar
Juniperus virginiana
varieties

'Canaertii': tree-like habit

With its crimson fruit, this stag's horn sumach (Rhus hirta 'Laciniata') creates an impressive display.

(16-23 ft; 5-7 m); large quantities of purple cones frosted with blue.

'Glauca': 16 ft (5 m) tall and 10-11 ft (3-3.5 m) wide; silvery grey foliage; round, brown-purple cones.

Position: neither variety is particular about soil or situation.

Yew
Taxus varieties
A squat, shrub-like tree with broadly spreading, somewhat upturned branches. The needles are dark green, and the red fruits contain poisonous seeds. The yew grows to 7-10 ft (2-3 m) in 10 years. Three varieties are noted for their particularly attractive berries:

T. baccata 'Fastigiata': columnar variety, growing to 10 ft (3 m).

T. b. 'Fastigiata Robusta': more erect habit than *T. b.* 'Fastigiata', with lighter-coloured needles.

T. media 'Hicksii': densely branching, with a loose columnar habit; grows very slowly up to 3-5 ft (1-1.5 m).

Position: sun to shade; lime-loving but robust; shade not necessary.

Maidenhair tree
Ginkgo biloba

Will grow to 13-20 ft (4-6 m) in 15 years. Leaves turn a beautiful yellow before falling. Yellow, plum-like fruit produced after warm seasons, ripening in autumn.

Shrubs that will grow in the shade

Shade-loving shrubs become increasingly useful as a garden becomes more mature. The plants in it grow together, and eventually there isn't enough daylight available for many sun-loving plants. By this stage you will need to concentrate more on those plants that flourish in the shade or semi-shade. Rhodo-dendrons, for example, will produce a fantastic display of flowers even in the shade.

Maple
Acer ginnala
Large shrub growing to 13-20 ft (4-6 m); the leaves turn to magnificent shades of red and orange in the autumn.

Flowers: end of May, yellowish-white, sweet-smelling.

Barberry
Berberis species and varieties

Dwarf forms: suitable for front gardens, rock gardens, low hedges and large tubs. They produce yellow flowers from April to May, and can tolerate most shade and soil conditions. They will put up with any kind of pruning, and even dry condi-tions. Examples include *B. can-didula* (2-3 ft; 60-100 cm) and *B.* 'Irwinii' (2-3 ft; 60-100 cm).

Larger forms: can be used for free-growing or clipped hedges,

or as solitaries: *B. gagnepainii lanceifolia* (7 ft; 2 m), *B. julianae* (7-10 ft; 2-3 m), *B. verruculosa* (3-5 ft; 1-1.5 m), with gently drooping branches. They produce yellow flowers like the dwarf forms, and are equally undemanding.

Common box
Buxus sempervirens
The variety of most interest to ordinary gardeners is 'Suffruti-cosa', which remains low-growing at around 24-31 in (60-80 cm). This classic edging plant is equally at home in a small cottage garden and in the parkland around a large country house. Prune it to the height you want in spring. If the leaves turn reddish, the plant isn't getting enough nutrients.

The velvet-leaved hydrangea (Hydrangea aspera sargentiana) bears parti-coloured blooms.

Hydrangea paniculata 'Grandiflora': the flowers are white at first, but gradually turn pink.

B. s. 'Bullata' and 'Handsworthiensis' will grow as high as 7–10 ft (2–3 m), which makes them more suitable as hedges. These slow-growing varieties have similar requirements to 'Suffruticosa'. 'Bullata' has puckered and blistered leaves.

Beauty berry
Callicarpa bodinieri 'Profusion'
A slow-growing shrub (5–7 ft; 1.5–2 m) with beautiful berries.

Flowers: July–August, lilac-coloured.

Fruits: pale, lilac-coloured berries like pearls, from September into the winter.

Position: sun to shade; protect from frost.

Care: prune only when damaged by frost.

Cornelian cherry
Cornus mas
This 16-ft (5-m) tall bush or small tree is particularly suitable for free-growing or clipped hedges. The foliage turns a lovely reddish-purple in autumn.

Flowers: February, yellow, attractive to bees.

Fruits: masses of red, cherry-like edible fruits from August.

Position: sun to shade; undemanding.

Care: prune as much as you like.

Red-barked dogwood
Cornus alba
Grows to 8–10 ft (2.5–3 m), and has red bark.

Position: sun or shade.

Care: don't prune if possible.

31

*The evergreen cherry laurel (*Prunus laurocerasus) *is also suitable for hedges.*

Recommended varieties and subspecies (giving leaf colour, followed by growth height of creeping and climbing forms respectively): 'Coloratus', green, 16 in (40 cm), 5 ft (1.5 m); 'Emerald Gaiety', white-edged, 8 in (20 cm), 3 ft (1 m); 'Emerald and Gold', yellow-variegated, 8 in (20 cm), 5 ft (1.5 m); 'Silver Queen', silvery-edged, 8 in (20 cm), 5 ft (1.5 m); 'Minimus', green, 6 in (15 cm), 20 in (50 cm); 'Radicans', green, 8 in (20 cm), 7 ft (2 m); *E. f. vegetus*, green, 2 ft (60 cm), 10 ft (3 m).

Position: sun to semi-shade.

Care: don't prune, just let it grow.

Common dogwood
Cornus sanguinea
Grows to 10 ft (3 m), with dark red or black bark, black fruit and dark red autumn colouring.

Position/care: as for *C. alba*.

Spindle tree
Euonymus europaeus
A 7-ft (2-m) tall shrub with pretty autumn colouring but insignificant flowers.

Fruits: conspicuous orange fruits with pink skins, eaten by birds but poisonous to humans.

Position: sun to semi-shade.

Care: thin out branches; renovation pruning possible.

Euonymus planipes
Grows to 7–10 ft (2–3 m), turning carmine red in the autumn; its flowers.are insignificant

Fruits: dark red fruits, beautiful but poisonous.

Position/care: as for spindle tree, but at its best in mild climates.

Euonymus fortunei
A creeping shrub that comes in many varieties. Will climb pebbledash walls, fences and climbing frames by means of aerial roots. Leaf colour and plant growth vary according to variety.

Tree ivy
Hedera 'Arborescens' varieties
Some of the ivies have free-standing varieties. Among the English ivy varieties, *H. helix* 'Arborescens', has a broad, bushy, upright habit and grows to 5 ft (1.5 m), while *H. h.* 'Arborescens Variegata' is similar but has larger leaves, variegated and patched creamy yellow.

Flowers: October, greenish-yellow.

Fruits: the following year, dark brown spherical berries.

Position: sun to shade.

Care: prune only to maintain the growth habit.

Hydrangea
Hydrangea

Hydrangeas are among the most beautiful of all flowering plants. They make an enormous difference to a garden, whatever the species or variety. Apart from the familiar hortensias, they include climbing forms and varieties with unusual flower structures:

H. arborescens 'Grandiflora'
A 2-m high shrub with a broad habit.

Flowers: July, flattened heads of creamy white flowers in great profusion.

Position: sun to shade; acid soil; sheltered location.

Care: remove dead flowers.

H. macrophylla and *H. serrata* hybrids
A group of thick, bushy shrubs growing to 3–7 ft (1–2 m). Similar to pot hydrangeas and available in several varieties.

Flowers: June–July, large, spherical heads of flowers. Colours vary according to variety: 'Bluebird' blue, 'Bouquet Rose' pink, 'Preziosa' crimson to purple, 'Rosalba' pink or blue.

Position: sun to shade; acid soil.

Care: remove dead flower heads in early spring; avoid drastic pruning as this will stop flowering.

Holly (Ilex) includes some varieties with brightly coloured leaves such as 'Golden King' and 'Golden van Tol'.

Velvet-leaved hydrangea
H. aspera sargentiana

This bushy shrub grows to 3–7 ft (1–2 m), and has dark green velvety leaves with downy undersides.

Flowers: July–August, distinctive flower heads with white flowers around the edges and violet flowers in the middle.

Position: sun to semi-shade; acid soil.

Care: prune as little as possible.

Climbing hydrangea
H. anomala petiolaris

A magnificent climbing shrub with reddish-brown shoots. It is self-clinging, and grows to 33 ft (10 m).

Flowers: June–July, large, loosely structured white flower heads.

Position: semi-shade to shade; damp, sandy, nutrient-rich soil.

Care: prune after the winter so that the flower heads grow larger; drastic pruning possible.

Holly
Ilex varieties

This slow-growing shrub or small tree (26–33 ft; 8–10 m) with its prickly leaves provides a rich harvest of red berries and a haven for birds. Varieties with patterned leaves are particularly recommended: *I. aquifolium* 'Argentea Marginata', slow-growing with white-edged

leaves; *I.* × *altaclerensis* 'Golden King', with broad yellow leaf margins; and *I. a.* 'Golden van Tol', with similarly yellow leaf margins. All are female.

Japanese holly
Ilex crenata
This low-growing holly (7-10 ft; 2-3 m) also grows slowly, but unlike the common holly (*I. aquifolium*) it has small leaves like those of the box, and its fruits are black. Of the varieties, 'Convexa' has spoon-shaped leaves, 'Golden Gem' turns yellow in the sun, and 'Stokes' grows to only 20 in (50 cm), with tiny leaves.

Position: sun to semi-shade.

Care: prune only when frost-damaged.

Jew's mallow
Kerria japonica
An undemanding shrub growing to 3-5 ft (1-1.5 m). The shoots die off every three years to give way to new growth. The 'Pleni-flora' variety, with its masses of double flowers, is more beautiful than the species,; it also grows faster, and achieves a greater height.

Flowers: April–June, double, deep yellow.

Position: full sun to semi-shade.

Care: thin out regularly.

Cherry laurel
Prunus laurocerasus
This densely growing shrub makes a good hedge with plenty

of privacy. It grows to around 5-8 ft (1.5-2.5 m) depending on the variety: 'Herbergii' 7 ft (2 m), upright habit; 'Otto Luyken' 3 ft (1 m), broad and bushy; 'Schipkaensis' 7-8 ft (2-2.5 m), loose, spreading habit, narrow leaves, free-flowering; 'Zabeliana' 31 in (80 cm), horizontally spreading branches.

Flowers: April–May, white spikes or clusters.

Fruits: black berries.

Position: sun to semi-shade; nutritious soil.

Care: avoid pruning.

Rhododendrons and azaleas
If you want to grow rhodo-dendrons, you have a bewilder-ing range of species, hybrids and varieties to choose from. To help you, we've classified them according to their origins and/or characteristics.

Large-flowered rhododendrons

These hybrids are worth having simply for their flowers, which are large or moderately large. There's an endless choice of colours ranging from white through yellow, pink, orange and red to deep violet. Varieties with a spot or 'eye' in the middle are especially popular.

The large-flowered hybrids grow to between 5 ft (1.5 m) and 11 ft (3.5 m), and are gen-

Above *The rhododendron year begins with the early-flowering* Rhododendron *'Praecox'.*

Left *Large-flowered rhododendrons need plenty of room for growth.*

erally as wide as they are tall. They can be grown in groups or as solitaries. The main flowering season is from April to mid-June.

R. insigne hybrids

These rhododendrons are prized for their dense, compact habit and strong, leathery, silver-backed leaves, which make them attractive even when they aren't in flower. They grow to only 3–5 ft (1–1.5 m) depending on the variety, so they're suitable for smaller gardens. The main flowering season is from late May to early June. But they

won't produce their bell-shaped flowers until they grow older.

R. forrestii Repens group

These dwarf rhododendrons reach no more than 16–39 in (40–100 cm), so are happy in small gardens, rock gardens or even tubs. They nearly all produce light or dark red flowers between April and May. Varieties such as 'Scarlet Wonder' and 'Bad Eilsen' bear attractive brownish-red buds in winter.

R. wardii hybrids

These attractive hybrids grow to between 4–8 ft (1.2–2.5 m), and are noted for their unusual yellow and pink flower shades. If you want yellow rhododendrons, then you must opt for this group. Main flowering season: May to early June.

Rhododendrons look good in combination with other plants — with these purple-flowered columbines, for example.

4-6 ft (1.2-1.8 m) depending on the variety, and produce large numbers of beautifully coloured blooms. These deciduous shrubs are also remarkably adaptable to different soils and positions. Nursery suppliers often divide azaleas into various subgroups such as the Knapp-Hill, *R. molle*, *R. occidentale*, *R. luteum* and *R.* × *rusticum* hybrids. The main flowering season is from May to June.

Wild species and their hybrids

This group includes the species that have not been specially bred and will therefore grow and flower naturally, as in the wild. Their small size (up to 3 ft; 1 m) and cushion-like habit makes them highly suitable for planting in tubs or troughs. The main flowering season is from spring into June, the exception being the March-flowering *R.* 'Praecox'.

Japanese azaleas

Often wrongly termed *R. japonica*, these plants are noted for their vast numbers of small but colourful blooms. They are small but bushy in habit, growing to no more than 3 ft (1 m), and can be planted in semi-shaded rock gardens or along the edges of footpaths and ponds. The leaves are evergreen, turning to a variety of colours in March.

R. williamsianum hybrids

This group lies somewhere between the large-flowered and the *R. forrestii* Repens group in terms of size, and will fit in small gardens or even tubs. Most of these hybrids will grow to 3-5 ft (1-1.5 m), although a few varieties reach 7-10 ft (2-3 m). They flower best in a sunny position, as shade tends to reduce budding. The main flowering season is from the end of April to the end of May.

R. yakushimanum hybrids

This group contains some particularly attractive forms. Most of them remain small (28-47 in;

70-120 cm), and the many varieties are noted for their dense clusters of magnificently coloured flowers. They grow slowly, and all of them come into flower as young plants. They tolerate sunlight well, often preferring a sunny position, which makes them suitable as tub plants or for sunny parts of the garden. These hybrids are perhaps the best choice for small or medium-sized gardens. The main flowering season lasts from May to June.

Azalea hybrids

In contrast to the evergreen rhododendrons, the azaleas generally drop their leaves in winter. They grow to between

During the main flowering season (from early May to early June) the leaves become invisible beneath a continuous carpet of flowers. The so-called diamond azaleas have an even more dwarf-like habit.

Planting and general care

Rhododendrons and azaleas thrive best in an acid soil with a pH level between 4.5 and 5.5. It's worth testing the pH level before you plant them: use one of the testing kits available from specialist shops or garden centres. If the pH is too high you should add some peat (or an environmentally friendly equivalent) in order to reduce it.

The soil where you plant should be lime-free, moisture-retentive, loose-structured and with plenty of humus. Dig out an area about three times as wide and twice as deep as the root ball of the plant. Then mix the soil you have dug out with 50–70 per cent of peat or equivalent, adding a sprinkling of lime-free stones of various sizes to ensure good drainage and ventilation. Make sure the root ball is really wet, and plant it flush with the ground. Leave an area clear around the plant so it can be watered easily.

Even if the soil has a lot of lime in it, this needn't stop you planting rhododendrons. You'll need to create a raised bed, held in by stones or pieces of wood, and fill it with a special rhododendron compost such as the ericaceous John Innes soil compost or a proprietary kind.

The best time to plant is between mid-September and the end of November, or from the beginning of March to the end of May. Before you put the plant in the hole, don't forget to remove the container. If the roots are balled in sacking, slit the sacking and remove the ball.

Feeding

Rhododendrons have only shallow roots, so they can't obtain enough nutrients on their own. This makes regular feeding essential, especially for large-flowered varieties. Wild species prefer organic fertilisers such as bonemeal or blood-fish-and-bone, while the large-flowered hybrids produce even better blooms if you use a special rhododendron fertiliser.

Apply the first feed in March or April. One recommended procedure is to give each plant a combination of 1.8 oz (50 g) of hoof-and-hornmeal and 3.5 oz (100 g) of rhododendron fertiliser. Spread the mixture thinly over the soil beneath the plant up to a distance of 10 in (25 cm) from the stem, then gently rake it into the soil.

It's worth applying a second feed in July, as this will ensure strong growth after the flowering period is over. This time you'll need only half the amount you used in spring.

Rhododendrons grow larger every year, and careful feeding will help them flower more readily.

Small-flowered rhododendrons, such as Japanese azaleas, some wild species and their hybrids, need less feeding than other forms. Use an organic fertiliser, giving less than half the normal amount.

Mulching

Rhododendrons will benefit greatly if you apply a 4-in (10-cm) layer of peat or pine-bark mulch to the surrounding soil, renewing the layer every 2–3 years. You could also cover the ground with leaf mould. The mulch layer helps to keep the soil moist.

Watering

The soil must always be kept sufficiently moist. If there is a long dry period, or the daytime temperature goes above 77°F (25°C), rhododendrons will need regular and plentiful watering, especially if they're standing alone. If the growing shoots start to go limp in the mornings, the plant is dying of thirst.

Garden sprays are often a good way to ensure a regular water supply.

Encouraging growth

Especially with young plants, it's a good idea to pull off the wilted flower-heads to prevent them from seeding. This encourages growth and also promotes the formation of new buds.

Plants that go well with rhododendrons

Solitary rhododendrons should be planted with companion plants that come into flower at a different time. These can be ground-cover species or foliage plants that greatly enhance the beauty of the rhododendron. Some lovely combinations can be achieved, rescuing the plant from its state of lonely isolation. Trees and shrubs can provide some much-needed shade in the midday sun, and will increase the humidity around the plant. Conifers may also give some shelter from the wind.

However, do take care to choose only plants with deep

roots. These won't compete with the shallow-rooted rhododendron for the water and nutrients in the soil. Companion trees should be pruned regularly to ensure good air circulation; you may even need to remove whole branches.

Suitable trees that won't compete for nutrients include

all indigenous pines, larches, maidenhair tree, sweet gum (*Liquidambar*), antarctic beech (*Nothofagus antarctica*) and laburnum. Possible shrubs include witch hazel, hortensia or hydrangea, or a red-leaved smoke tree, and a flowering dogwood (*Cornus florida*) is almost compulsory. The reddish autumn colouring of *Enkianthus campanulatus* goes well with rhododendrons, as do star magnolia, *Magnolia sieboldii*, and the Japanese snowball (*Viburnum plicatum* 'Mariesii').

Alpine currant
Ribes alpinum 'Schmidt'
This 3–7-ft (1–2-m) high shrub has gently drooping branches and is suitable for hedges. It starts growing early, and is late to shed its leaves.

Flowers: from April, greenish-yellow.

Fruits: inedible berries.

Position: sun to semi-shade, but avoid direct sun or dryness.

Care: renovation pruning desirable every 2–3 years.

Common elder
Sambucus nigra
A 16-ft (5-m) tall shrub that provides food for birds.

Fruits: June–August, black berries that can be cooked or used for elderberry juice.

Evergreen rhododendrons always look much more attractive when combined with a selection of deciduous varieties.

Flowers: large white clusters of aromatic flowers.

Position: sun to semi-shade; humus-rich soil with plenty of nutrients.

Care: will tolerate even drastic pruning.

American elder
Sambucus canadensis 'Maxima'
Grows to 10–13 ft (3–4 m).

Flowers: like common elder, but flower heads very large.

Fruits: from August, purple-red edible berries.

Position/care: see common elder.

Snowberry and coralberry
Symphoricarpos
These undemanding shrubs produce flowers that are popular with bees, while the snow-white or coral-red berries are much prized by gardeners. They remain on the bush until well into the winter, for the simple reason that the birds don't eat them. On the other hand, snowberry hedges make popular nesting sites.

S. **'White Hedge'** grows to 5 ft (1.5 m), with strongly upright shoots. It's better suited to gardens than the true snowberry (*S. albus* var. *laevigatus*), which grows to 7 ft (2 m) and tends to run wild. 'White Hedge' also has much larger white fruits, which appear in September and stay on the bush for a long time.

S. × *chenaultii* '**Hancock**' is a flat, spreading variety (20–30 in; 50–80 cm) that provides excellent ground cover but don't combine it with other dwarf shrubs.

S. '**Magic Berry**' grows to 30 in (80 cm), and develops a dense, broad habit. It bears enormous, lilac-red berries, and we recommend it for low hedges.

S. '**Variegatus**' grows to 5 ft (1.5 m) with a graceful habit; it has smaller leaves than most, but they have irregular yellow margins; it needs light to maintain the variegation.

Position: sun to semi-shade; suits all garden soils.

Care: no problems with pruning.

Guelder rose
Viburnum opulus 'Roseum'
The ever-popular guelder rose grows to 10–13 ft (3–4 m) and has a densely branching habit.

Flowers: May–June, large white 'snowballs' of densely double flowers.

Position: dappled sun to semi-shade, but no intense sunlight.

Care: regular thinning advisable.

Conifers

Dwarf Hinoki cypress
Chamaecyparis obtusa 'Nana Gracilis'
Slow-growing (3–7 ft; 1–2 m) and noted for its strangely twisted branches.

Position: bright to semi-shaded, but doesn't like intense sunlight.

Yew
Taxus baccata
A squat, shrub-like tree with broadly spreading upturned branches, the yew has dark green needles and red berries with poisonous seeds. It grows to 3–7 ft (2–3 m) in 10 years, and comes in many interesting varieties.

The following varieties are broader than they are tall: 'Nissen's Corona' 13–16 ft (4–5 m) wide; 'Nissen's Dirigent' 10–13 ft (3–4 m); 'Nissen's Kadett' 16–20 ft (5–6 m); 'Nissen's Praesident' 13–16 ft (4–5 m).

Westfelton yew (*T. b.* 'Dovastoniana'): a small tree or shrub (5–7 ft; 1.5–2 m) with horizontally spreading, slightly drooping branches.

Position: sun to shade; sturdy, lime-loving plants.

This dwarf Hinoki cypress (Chamaecyparis obtusa 'Nana Gracilis') is particularly suitable for tubs and rock gardens.

Columnar varieties of yew

T. b. **'Fastigiata':** forms thin columns up to 10 ft (3 m) in height.

T. b. **'Fastigiata Robusta':** this yew is of more erect habit than *T. b.* 'Fastigiata', and it also has lighter-green needles.

T. b. **'Overeynderi':** a slower-growing variety with a more spherical habit; a suitable hedge plant.

T. × media **'Hicksii':** a hybrid yew of loose columnar habit without a central shoot; densely branching and very slow-growing, eventually reaching 3-5 ft; (1-1.5 m).

Position: sun to shade; sturdy, lime-loving plants.

Low-growing forms of yew

T. b. **'Repandens':** a broad, spreading conifer 12-20 in (30-50 cm) high and 7-10 ft (2-3 m) wide, with a regular growth habit.

Japanese yew (*T. cuspidata nana*): a low-growing shrub subspecies with widely spreading branches, growing up to 3 ft (1 m) high and as much as 7 ft (2 m) wide.

Position: sun to semi-shade; lime-tolerant, likes any soil, extremely frost-hardy.

Common hemlock
Tsuga canadensis

A medium-sized tree growing to 10-13 ft (3-4 m) — taller after 15 years. Common hemlock has a loose habit, often with multiple stems. Two particular varieties are recommended:

T. c. **'Nana':** a dwarf variety, growing to only 12-16 in (30-40 cm) in height, and 20-30 in (50-80 cm) wide — larger after 15 years.

T. c. **'Pendula':** grows to 3 ft (1 m) tall and 7 ft (2 m) wide, with

Taxus baccata 'Fastigiata' is a columnar yew that grows to about 10 ft (3 m) in 10 years.

low-hanging branches and an irregular growth habit.

Position: sun to semi-shade; prefers acid soils; sensitive to heat and dryness, so avoid southerly aspects.

Particularly fast-growing shrubs

Some trees and shrubs, including many of the flowering varieties, grow more than 3 ft (1 m) a year in their first few years.

Broadleaves

Box elder
Acer negundo cultivars
Tall, fast-growing shrubs with a loose habit, reaching 16–23 ft (5–7 m), and including several varieties with fascinating leaf patterns.

Varieties: 'Aureovariegatum', yellow-variegated foliage; 'Flamingo', leaves with light pink margins, later developing white variegations; 'Variegatum', leaves with white or variegated edges, preceded (March–April) by yellowish-white flowers.

Position: sun to semi-shade.

Care: no unnecessary pruning, but remove reversions (shoots with green leaves).

Birches
Betula
Birches are chiefly prized for their brilliant white bark and loosely growing branches. The multi-stemmed forms are particularly attractive (and expensive). Birches create great problems for all neighbouring plants, because they extract all the water and nutrients from the soil, so you should normally limit yourself to dwarf forms. Tall-growing birches are only suitable for large gardens, where they make very attractive solitaries.

*Young's weeping birch (*Betula pendula *'Youngii') is a solitary plant that needs plenty of space.*

B. pendula 'Fastigiata': a narrow, columnar variety of birch that grows to 33–50 ft (10–15 m).

Monarch birch (*B. maximowicziana*): grows to 49 ft (15 m), and the bronze-coloured bark makes it the most attractive of all birches.

Arctic birch (*B. nana*): a spreading dwarf species, 20 in (50 cm) high and 7 ft (2 m) wide; suitable for rock or heather gardens.

Young's weeping birch (*B. pendula* 'Youngii'): a weeping variety, growing to 10 ft (3 m),

with drooping branches that hang down to the ground.

Position: sunny to well lit; sensitive to lime.

Care: prune sparingly; best when planted before spring growth begins.

Indian bean tree
Catalpa bignonioides
This 33–50-ft (10–15-m) tall tree has pretty flower clusters and interesting fruit, but except for the dwarf variety *C. b.* 'Nana' it is usually suitable only for large gardens, or as a solitary.

Flowers: June–July, covered with clusters of white flowers.

Fruit: from September, long brown pods measuring some 16 in (40 cm).

Position: sunny, but won't tolerate dryness.

Care: prune sparingly, preferably only where damaged by frost.

Crab apple
Malus
Ornamental crab apples are noted for their glorious late spring blossoms (May–June) and their decorative autumn fruits. The flowers may be single or double, varying in colour from white through pink to orange, scarlet, wine-red or purple. The many varieties are available as

Above *Indian bean tree (Catalpa bignonioides)*

Below *Crab apples (Malus species and varieties) come in a variety of shrubby and standard forms.*

43

Crab apples (Malus) can be red, yellow or orange in colour.

Ornamental cherries
Prunus species and varieties
Flowering trees and shrubs of various shapes, capable of producing glorious displays of blossoms.

Flowers: the season varies from March to June according to the variety ('Autumnalis' flowers from late autumn to March); colour mainly white, with pink or red tints.

Position: sunny or well lit, likes deep, porous, loosely structured soil.

Care: avoid pruning in case the sap runs, but saw off sick or overgrown branches just before the leaves are shed.

False acacia
Robinia
Gardens just don't have enough space for the false acacia or locust tree (*R. pseudoacacia*). This fast-growing species simply gets too big, and the suckers can be a real nuisance. However, the following closely related varieties can be accommodated in a larger garden:

Mop-head acacia (*R. pseudo-acacia* 'Umbraculifera'): a small tree (13 ft; 4 m) that grows into a spherical habit without any pruning.

***R. pseudoacacia* 'Tortuosa':** a slow-growing, medium-sized tree (26–33 ft; 8–10 m) with corkscrew-like branches and leaves. It bears long clusters of fragrant white flowers in June.

standards (13–33 ft; 4–10 m) or as shrubs. We strongly recommend the shrubs.

Position: full sun to dappled shade.

Care: don't prune except to thin out branches after the winter.

Antarctic beech
Nothofagus antarctica
A small tree (16–23 ft; 5–7 m) with several main stems and a loose habit. The leaves turn golden yellow in the autumn.

Flowers: April–May, insignificant.

Position: full sun to dappled shade.

Care: don't prune.

Foxglove tree
Paulownia tomentosa
A medium-sized tree, growing to 33–50 ft (10–15 m) as it matures. Needs a solitary position in a large garden, and a sheltered, sunny site.

Flowers: May, 12-in (30-cm) tall clusters of light purple, foxglove-like flowers.

Position: sun to semi-shade, lime-loving.

Care: young plants tolerate pruning, older plants less so.

Cherry plum
Prunus cerasifera 'Nigra'
A small tree or large shrub (16 ft; 5 m) with drooping branches and deep purple leaves. Good with white-flowering shrubs.

Flowers: from April, pink.

Fruits: edible, pleasant-tasting.

Position: sun to semi-shade.

Care: pruning possible but not necessary.

Rose acacia (*R. hispida* 'Macrophylla'): an upright-growing shrub (5–8 ft; 1.5–2.5 m) that produces attractive clusters of rose-red flowers from June onwards.

Position: sunny or well lit.

Care: don't prune.

Willows
Salix

There are many species and varieties of willow that interest gardeners, including the many dwarf, weeping or creeping forms, and those with decorative catkins.

Willows with unusually attractive catkins

Violet willow
S. daphnoides
This large shrub (16–26 ft; 5–8 m) has purple bark with a bluish-white bloom.

Flowers: from February; very long, silvery white catkins.

Position: sunny or well lit.

Care: pruning possible.

S. × smithiana
A 16–20-ft (5–6-m) tall shrub that is popular with bees.

Flowers: March–April; dense clusters of yellow catkins.

Position: sunny or well lit.

Care: pruning recommended.

Goat willow
S. caprea mas
A flowering shrub that grows to 10–13-ft (3–4-m).

Flowers: February–March; male catkins yellow and unusually large; female catkins silvery and furry, known as pussy willow.

Position: sunny or well lit.

Care: pruning possible.

S. 'Silberglanz'
This winter-flowering willow grows to 13 ft (4 m) and forms elegantly drooping branches.

Flowers: from Nov–Dec onwards; silvery white catkins, multiplying from March onwards, when they turn golden yellow.

Position: sunny or well lit.

Care: pruning possible.

Willows with an unusual habit

Weeping goat willow
S. caprea 'Pendula'
A 7-ft (2-m) high shrub with branches that hang down vertically to the ground.

Flowers: yellow catkins in particularly dense clusters.

Position: sunny or well lit.

Care: prune the flower shoots after they have finished flowering.

S. udensis 'Sekka'
A 10-ft (3-m) tall shrub with weirdly spreading branches.

Flowers: April, yellow catkins.

Position: open but not sunny.

Care: thinning desirable.

Salix caprea *'Pendula' will fit in even the smallest of gardens.*

Corkscrew willow
S. 'Tortuosa'
This 20-ft (6-m) high tree grows slowly, and is remarkable for its weirdly deformed and twisted branches and leaves.

Flowers: April, yellow male catkins.

Salix 'Sekka' is a Japanese variety of willow whose unusual features can best be appreciated if it is standing on its own.

Position: sunny or well lit.

Care: don't prune if at all possible.

Dwarf or creeping willows

Suitable for low hedges, large rock gardens, dry stone walls and other hanging positions.

Dwarf purple osier
S. purpurea 'Nana'
A round bush growing to 20–40 in (50–100 cm) in height, with pretty silvery grey leaves, purplish shoots, and reddish-coloured catkins in March and April.

Silver creeping willow
S. repens argentea
This ground-cover shrub grows no higher than 12–20 in (30–50 cm), and bears yellow catkins in April; its leaves are silvery.

Common elder
Sambucus nigra
A 16-ft (5-m) tall shrub that provides food for birds.

Flowers: clusters of large, white, aromatic flowers.

Fruits: June–August, black berries that can be cooked or juiced.

Position: sun to semi-shade; humus-rich soil with plenty of nutrients.

Care: will tolerate even drastic pruning.

Mountain ash, rowan
Sorbus aucuparia
This popular fruit tree species grows to 25 ft (8 m), so it's best in medium to large gardens. The red berries are edible; they're also rich in vitamin C.

'Edulis' has fruits twice the size of the species, making it the ideal choice if you want to eat the fruit.

'Fastigiata' is a smaller, columnar variety, growing to only 16 ft (5 m).

Position: sunny or well lit.

Care: pruning is not recommended.

The bright red fruits of the mountain ash (Sorbus aucuparia) *provide a feast for many of our songbirds.*

Conifers

Blue cedar
Cedrus libani atlantica
Glauca group
Grows to 33–49 ft (10–15 m) and has lovely silver-blue needles. After 10 years it produces many cones right down to the lowest branches.

C. l. a. '**Glauca Pendula**' is the weeping form of the blue cedar, with branches hanging vertically down to the ground. It varies in height, but still has silvery blue needles. It works best as a solitary in a large or medium-sized garden.

Position: sun to semi-shade; intolerant of lime-rich soils.

Himalayan cedar, deodar
Cedrus deodara
Grows to 33–49 ft (10–15 m), with elegantly drooping branches and long, flexible bright green needles.

Larches
Larix
Only suitable for large gardens, parks and woodland estates. All larches shed their needles in autumn.

European larch (*L. decidua*): grows to 80–100 ft (25–30 m), with horizontal or slightly drooping branches.

Japanese larch (*L. kaempferi*): grows to 50–65 ft (15–20 m), with horizontal branches and bluish-green needles.

L. kaempferi '**Pendula**': the weeping form of the Japanese larch is not as tall as the upright-growing species. As it grows only very slowly, it will fit nicely in a medium-sized garden.

Position: sun to semi-shade; likes cool, damp conditions, but sensitive to environmental pollution.

Serbian spruce
Picea omorika
Although it is 50 ft (15 m) tall, this tree has a decidedly columnar habit, so it will fit in a medium-sized garden.

Position: sun to semi-shade; very sturdy.

Douglas fir
Pseudotsuga menziesii f. *caesia*
Suitable only for large gardens or parks; grows fast to 20–26 ft (6–8 m), and eventually reaches 80–100 ft (25–30 m) as it grows older; grey-green foliage.

Position: sun to semi-shade; extremely hardy; unsuitable for urban gardens.

Ground-cover shrubs to help keep the soil moist and prevent weeds growing

As well as providing ground cover and easing the gardener's workload (useful enough in itself), these plants can often be highly decorative, producing flowers for months on end.

Broadleaves

Evergreen barberry
Berberis varieties
The various dwarf evergreen forms make good ground-cover plants, and are also suitable for low hedges, edging and large tubs. Some of the best ground-cover varieties include *B.* 'Corallina' (up to 3 ft; 1 m), *B. buxifolia* 'Nana' (12 in; 30 cm), *B. candidula* (2-3 ft; 60-100 cm) and *B.* 'Irwinii' (2-3 ft; 60-100 cm).

Flowers: April–May, yellow ('Corallina' has red buds, opening yellow).

Position: sun to semi-shade.

Care: undemanding; will tolerate any kind of pruning.

Ling, heather
Calluna vulgaris cultivars
The most interesting of these summer-flowering heathers are the varieties that grow to 8-24 in (20-60 cm) and flower between August and September. In the case of 'Annemarie', 'H. E. Beale' and 'Peter Sparkes' the

pink flowers don't appear until September or October. 'Aurea' has purple flowers and yellow foliage that turns bronze-coloured in winter, and 'Gold Haze' has white flowers and yellow foliage all year round.

Position: sun to semi-shade, no lime.

Care: prune a little every other year, after flowering or early in spring.

Creeping cotoneasters
Cotoneaster varieties
C. × *suecicus* 'Cardinal': 12-16 in (30-40 cm) high; lovely autumn colouring; large white flowers (May–June); red fruits.
C. radicans 'Eichholz': 10 in (25 cm) high, 20 in (50 cm) wide,

creeping; white flowers (May–June); red fruits. *C. ×
suecicus* 'Coral Beauty': 10 in (25 cm) high; white flowers
(June); large, persistent, coral-red fruits. *C. dammeri radicans*:
4 in (10 cm) high, very flat-growing; whitish-red flowers
(May–June); very large, bright red fruits. *C. procumbens*: 4–6 in
(10–15 cm) high, 12 in (30 cm) wide, very slow-growing; white
flowers (May–June); red fruits. *C. salicifolius* 'Parkteppich':

Above *Some varieties of shrubby
cinquefoil (*Potentilla fruticosa*) have
white or yellow flowers.*

Left *Creeping wintergreen (*Gaultheria procumbens*) is one of our most
valuable ground-cover plants.*

12–16 in (30–40 cm) high; large
white flowers (May–June);
bright red fruits.

Heath
Erica carnea hybrids
Most of these are low-growing,
evergreen ground-cover shrubs,
growing no higher than 8 in (20
cm), and suitable for heather
gardens and containers. The
flowering season and flower
colours vary depending on the
variety.

Varieties: 'Alba': white flowers,
January–April, 10 in (25 cm).
'Atrorubra': carmine red,
March–May, 8 in (20 cm).

'Myretoun Ruby': bright red,
March–May, 6 in (15 cm).
'Snow Queen': pure white,
January–April, 8 in (20 cm).
'Vivellii': violet-red, March–
April, 8 in (20 cm). 'Winter
Beauty': pink, December–
March, 6–8 in (15–20 cm).

Position: sunny or well lit,
lime-loving.

Care: prune lightly after
flowering.

Euonymus fortunei
This creeping shrub makes a
good ground-cover plant, but its
aerial roots also enable it to
climb pebbledash walls, fences
and climbing frames. Leaf
colour and plant growth vary
according to variety.

Recommended varieties
(giving leaf colour, followed by
growth height of creeping and
climbing forms respectively):

49

'Coloratus', green, 16 in (40 cm), 5 ft (1.5 m); 'Emerald Gaiety', white-edged, 8 in (20 cm), 3 ft (1 m); 'Emerald and Gold', yellow-variegated, 8 in (20 cm), 5 ft (1.5 m); 'Variega-tus', silvery-edged, 8 in (20 cm), 5 ft (1.5 m); 'Minimus', green, 6 in (15 cm), 20 in (50 cm); *E. f. radicans*, green, 8 in (20 cm), 7 ft (2 m); *E. f. vegetus*, green, 2 ft (60 cm), 10 ft (3 m).

Position: sun to semi-shade.

Care: don't prune, just let it grow.

Creeping wintergreen
Gaultheria procumbens
A slow-growing dwarf shrub (4–8 in; 10–20 cm) with beautiful berries and leathery leaves that turn reddish in the autumn.

Flowers: June–August, small, whitish.

Fruits: spherical red berries.

Position: sun to semi-shade; humus-rich soil with plenty of nutrients.

Care: no pruning.

Broom
Genista
The true brooms are small but very strong-willed plants, none of which grow higher than 32 in (80 cm).

G. lydia: 12–20 in (30–50 cm), yellow flowers (May–June).

G. sagittalis: 8–12 in (20–30 cm) high and twice as wide, with winged stems and golden yellow flowers (June–July).

Dyer's greenweed (*G. tinctoria* 'Flore Pleno'): 12–20 in (30–50 cm); a creeping shrub with conspicuous yellow double flowers (June–September).

English ivy
Hedera helix
Creeps continuously, spreading quickly and rooting immediately. Climbs up to 66 ft (20 m) using aerial roots; otherwise no higher than 8 in (20 cm).

Flowers: October, greenish-yellow.

Fruits: black berries the following year.

Position: sun to shade.

Care: only prune to maintain the growth habit.

Honeysuckle
Lonicera species and varieties
Honeysuckles come in many different forms, including upright, creeping and twining species. The upright forms are often grown as flowering hedges. Among the best ground-cover forms are:

L. pileata: 16 in (40 cm) high, 30–40 in (80–100 cm) wide, creeping habit; flowers and fruits hidden by foliage.

L. × xylosteoides 'Clavey's Dwarf': up to 3 ft (1 m) high, with insignificant flowers and fruit.

Position: sun to semi-shade.

Care: thin out constantly, removing dead shoots; reacts badly to renovation pruning.

*This garden is covered with the rose-pink flowers of a Japanese spiraea (*Spiraea japonica *'Little Princess').*

Shrubby cinquefoil
Potentilla fruticosa varieties
A small, thick, bushy shrub that
grows to between 16 in (40 cm)
and 5 ft (1.5 m), depending on
the variety. It's noted for its long
flowering period.

Flowers: May–October non-
stop; flowers immediately after
planting.

Position: sun to semi-shade;
robust but sensitive to heat and
dryness; no lime.

Care: prune and thin regularly
to encourage flowering.

Recommended varieties:
'Elizabeth': light yellow flowers
(Jun–Sep), 24–31 in (60–80 cm)
tall. 'Goldkugel': dark yellow
(Jun–Sep), 24–40 in (60–100
cm). 'Goldfinger': lemon yellow
(Jun–Aug), 3–7 ft (1–2 m).
'Hachmanns Gigant': golden
yellow (Jun–Sep), 20–28 in
(50–70 cm). 'Klondike': light
yellow (Jun–Aug), 3–4 ft (1–1.2
m). 'Red Ace': reddish inside,
yellow outside (Jun–Jul), 16–24
in (40–60 cm).

Japanese spiraea
Spiraea japonica 'Little
Princess'
This low-growing shrub (16 in;
40 cm) makes an excellent
ground-cover plant.

Flowers: July–August, clusters
of small rose-pink flowers.

Position: sunny or dappled
shade.

Care: prune back vigorously
every spring.

Conifers

Creeping junipers
Juniperus varieties
The creeping forms of juniper
include *J. communis* 'Horni-
brookii', *J. c.* 'Repanda', *J. hori-
zontalis glauca* and *J. sabina*
'Tamariscifolia'. No higher than
12 in (30 cm), they all form
carpets or cushions measuring
3–5 ft (1–1.5 m) across, depending on the variety.

Position: sun to semi-shade;
robust; tolerates fairly dry soils.

Microbiota decussata
This creeping evergreen shrub
grows 8–12 in (20–30 cm) high
and 3–5 ft (1–1.5 m) wide. Its
needles turn brownish in winter.

*Creeping junipers (Juniperus
communis varieties) make robust
ground-cover plants for the sun or
semi-shade.*

Position: sun to shade; robust;
tolerates dryness.

Dwarf pine
Pinus mugo pumilio
This tiny shrub spreads out to
form green cushions 20–24 in
(50–60 cm) high and 30–40 in
(80–100 cm) wide.

Position: sunny.

Spreading yew
Taxus baccata 'Repandens'
Grows to 12–20 in (30–50 cm)
high and 7–10 ft (2–3 m) wide,
with a regular habit.

Position: sun to shade (optional).

Shrubs suitable for informal flowering hedges that don't need trimming

Free-growing hedges can be a stable and highly attractive feature in any garden. They also give you privacy; but if you don't want to use shears on them, you must give them plenty of space to sprawl.

Serviceberry
Amelanchier laevis
This beautiful flowering shrub grows to 8–10 ft (2.5–3 m) in height. The multiple stems bear red shoots, and the leaves turn orange in the autumn. The closely related *A. lamarckii* grows to 13 ft (4 m) and has smaller flowers.

Flowers: April, white, hanging in 5-in (12-cm) long clusters.

Fruits: edible, dark red berries.

Position: sunny or well lit.

Care: thin out after flowering, otherwise no pruning.

Butterfly bush
Buddleia davidii hybrids
This shrub will grow in any garden, and is a magnet for butterflies. It grows to between 7 ft (2 m) and 10 ft (3 m) depending on the variety, and

provides an excellent source of food for insects. There are several varieties, with flowers ranging in colour from white through pink and purple to deep violet.

Flowers: between July and October, depending on the variety; sweet-smelling.

Position: sunny or dappled shade.

Care: shorten the soft shoot tips in the autumn, and in spring cut back the previous year's flowered shoots.

Flowering quince, japonica
Chaenomeles speciosa
Grows to 7–10 ft (2–3 m) and bears bright red flowers from March to April. The edible fruits are yellowish-green tinged with red, and appear from August onwards.

Position: sunny or dappled shade; likes most soils and tolerates dryness.

Care: can be trimmed as a hedge; thin out occasionally.

This serviceberry (Amelanchier lamarckii) would be a gift to any garden.

Cornelian cherry
Cornus mas
A 16-ft (5-m) tall flowering shrub or small tree, suitable for free-growing or clipped hedges. The leaves turn red–purple in autumn.

Flowers: February, yellow, attractive to bees.

Fruits: lots of red, cherry-like edible fruits from August on.

Position: sun to semi-shade; undemanding.

Care: copes with any pruning.

Cotoneasters
Cotoneaster species

Cotoneaster franchettii is a semi-evergreen shrub (5–7 ft; 1.5–2 m) with long, drooping branches and gorgeous-coloured fruit. It bears white or reddish flowers from June onwards, followed in August by a long-lasting display of bright orange-red berries.

Cotoneaster multiflorus is deciduous, and is much taller (7–10 ft; 2–3 m) with a dense, bushy habit. White flowers in May are followed by bright red berries in July.

Position: sun to semi-shade.

Care: young plants can be pruned vigorously; afterwards prune sparingly.

Deutzia
Deutzia × magnifica
A magnificent flowering shrub that grows to 10 ft (3 m) and has an upright habit.

*The flowering quince (*Chaenomeles speciosa*) has pretty flowers and thorny shoots, and its fruits are edible.*

Flowers: pure white, in 5-in (12-cm) long clusters.

Position: sunny or dappled shade; doesn't like dryness.

Care: thin out every 2–3 years.

Forsythia
Forsythia varieties
This shrub comes into flower in March or April, and is a must for any garden. It works better as a free-growing or clipped hedge than as a solitary, and grows to between 3 ft (1 m) and 10 ft (3 m) depending on the variety.

The most attractive varieties: 'Beatrix Ferrand', dark yellow flowers, 10 ft (3 m) high; 'Goldzauber', golden yellow, 5–7 ft (1.5–2 m); 'Minigold', light yellow, 3–5 ft (1–1.5 m); 'Spring Glory', light yellow, 7–10 ft (2–3 m); 'Tetragold', deep yellow, 3–5 ft (1–1.5 m).

Position: full sun to dappled shade.

Care: thin out every two to three years; renovation pruning needed for older plants.

53

of forms, including upright (grown as flowering hedges), ground-cover and climbing or twining species:

L. involucrata ledebourii: 7-10 ft (2-3 m) tall; broad, bushy habit; yellowish-red flowers in June.

L. maackii: 10-13 ft (3-4 m) tall, with umbrella-shaped crowns; yellow autumn colouring; masses of whitish-yellow flowers in June; poisonous red berries.

Jew's mallow
Kerria japonica
This undemanding shrub grows to between 3 ft (1 m) and 5 ft (1.5 m). The shoots die off every three years to allow new growth. The 'Pleniflora' variety is more attractive than the species, and also grows taller and more vigorously.

Flowers: April–June, double in 'Pleniflora', deep yellow.

Position: full sun to semi-shade.

Care: thin out regularly.

Beauty bush
Kolkwitzia amabilis
A strongly branching shrub that grows to 7-10 ft (2-3 m), highly

Above *This variety of Jew's mallow (Kerria japonica 'Pleniflora') will flower for as long as 4 to 6 weeks.*

Right *The pink blossoms of the beauty bush (Kolkwitzia amabilis) are striking even from a distance.*

recommended for its rich floral display; 'Pink Cloud' is the best cultivar.

Flowers: May–June, large, pink clusters.

Position: sun to semi-shade.

Care: thin out carefully so as not to reduce flowering.

Honeysuckle
Lonicera species
Honeysuckles come in a variety

L. tatarica: 10-13 ft (3-4 m) tall; starts growing early; white to pink flowers in May–June; poisonous light red berries.

Fly honeysuckle (*L. xylosteum*): 8 ft (2.5 m) tall; slower growing and less vigorous than *L. tatarica*; yellowish-white flowers from May onwards; poisonous dark red berries.

Position: sun to semi-shade.

Care: thin out constantly, removing dead shoots; will even tolerate renovation pruning.

Philadelphus

A group of undemanding shrubs with beautiful flowers, growing to between 3 ft (1 m) and 10 ft (3 m) depending on the species or variety.

Flowers: May–July, white, sweet-smelling; single, semi-double or double.

Position: sun to shade, but produces fewer flowers in the shade; undemanding.

Care: feed regularly in the spring; prune after flowering, thinning out older plants; drastic pruning possible.

Mock orange, syringa (*P. coronarius*): grows to 10 ft (3 m), single flowers, ideal for hedges.

Recommended varieties: 'Erectus': single flowers, heavily scented, 5-7 ft (1.5-2 m); *P. inodorus grandiflorus*: single bell-shaped flowers, up to 13 ft (4 m); 'Boule d'Argent': dense clusters of double flowers, slightly fragrant, 5-6 ft (1.5-2 m); 'Virginal': double flowers, strongly fragrant, 7-10 ft (2-3 m).

Shrubby cinquefoil

Potentilla fruticosa species and varieties
These small, bushy shrubs grow to between 16 in (40 cm) and 5 ft (1.5 m) depending on the variety, and are noted for their long flowering period. The two varieties 'Goldfinger' (4-7 ft; 1.2-2 m) and 'Klondike' (3-7 ft; 1-2 m) are particularly suitable for hedges, as is the original species *P. fruticosa*.

Flowers: May–October non-stop; flowers immediately after planting.

Position: sun to semi-shade; any well-drained soil; robust.

Care: must be pruned and thinned regularly to encourage flowering.

Flowering currant
Ribes sanguineum varieties

'Atrorubens' grows to 5-7 ft (1.5-2 m) with a loose upright habit, and produces clusters of dark red flowers from April on. The fruit is not pleasant to eat.

'King Edward VII' is weaker growing and has crimson flowers.

Position: sun or dappled shade; any soil.

Care: renovation pruning every 2-3 years; prune after flowering.

Spiraea
The spring-flowering forms of these shrubs are a must for any garden, whether as solitaries or as flowering hedges. Their branches are weighed down almost to the ground by masses of snow-white blooms.

Foam of May, bridal wreath (*S. × arguta*) grows slowly to 5-7 ft (1.5-2 m) with an upright habit. The clusters of white flowers appear in April on the previous year's shoots.

S. prunifolia grows to 7 ft (2 m), with an upright habit and long, drooping branches. It produces a magnificent display of white double flowers from April to May.

S. × vanhouttei grows to 7 ft (2 m) with heavily drooping branches. From May to June it is simply covered with white flowers.

Position: sunny or dappled shade.

Care: thin out regularly to encourage new growth.

Lilac
Syringa vulgaris cultivars
Lilacs come in various bushy or standard forms. The fragrant blossoms appear in May, and may be either single or double depending on the variety.

Single varieties: 'Souvenir de Louis Späth', dark purple; 'Primrose', primrose yellow.

Double varieties: 'Charles Joly', purplish-red with lighter-coloured flower tips; 'Katharine Havemeyer', lilac to purplish-pink, densely semi-double; 'Michel Buchner', lilac with a white 'eye'; 'Madame Lemoine', pure white; 'Mrs Edward Harding', purplish-red to purplish-pink.

Position: sunny or well lit, but never in shade or semi-shade;

This hybrid spiraea (Spiraea × vanhouttei) presents a magnificent display of flowers.

prefers a well-drained, humus-rich soil.

Care: thin out after flowering; cut out bare branches; tolerates renovation pruning.

Rouen lilac
Syringa × chinensis
This thick, bushy shrub grows to 10 ft (3 m) with drooping branches, and produces large, pendulous clusters of lilac-coloured flowers from May to June. The less vigorous 'Saugeana' variety (7 ft; 2 m) has darker, more purple-hued flowers.

Position: sun or semi-shade; sensitive to dryness.

Care: if possible avoid pruning, although it will tolerate renovation; carefully remove all dead flowers.

Guelder rose
Viburnum opulus 'Roseum'
This popular shrub grows to 10–13 ft (3–4 m) with a densely branching habit.

Flowers: May–June, large white 'snowballs' of densely double flowers.

Position: dappled sun to semi-shade.

Care: regular thinning advisable.

Japanese snowball
Viburnum plicatum
Grows to 7–8 ft (2–2.5 m) in height, but is wider than it is tall.

Flowers: May–June, white, often lasting as long as a month.

Position: sun to semi-shade.

Care: pruning not necessary, but remove ailing shoots.

Weigela
Weigela hybrids
The best weigelas are the hybrids because their flowers are so lovely. These broad, bushy shrubs grow to between 5–10 ft (1.5–3 m).

Varieties: 'Bristol Ruby': carmine red flowers, May–June; 'Eva Rathke': carmine red, June–August; 'Newport Red': deep red, June–July.

Position: sun to semi-shade.

The guelder rose with its large white pompoms lends a touch of nostalgia to a garden.

Care: thin out every 2–3 years; drastic pruning possible.

Lilac has a reputation for being easy to please, but this shouldn't stop you from feeding it regularly. Give it some rotted garden compost in the spring, and apply an organic fertiliser from July onwards (about 2 oz/sq yd or 70–80 g/m^2).

Columnar varieties of conifer

Columnar forms of conifer are something special, so they should never be hidden among a crowd of trees or other taller-growing shrubs. It's best to plant them as solitaries, or in the company of smaller plants such as roses, wild perennials or grasses. Other possible locations include heather gardens and large troughs.

Lawson cypress
Chamaecyparis lawsoniana varieties

'**Alumii**': forms columns 16–23 ft (5–7 m) tall, has steel-blue sprays of foliage, and also makes a good hedge plant. 'Alumii' is generally undemanding, preferring a moderately dry to damp soil, and likes a sunny or semi-shaded location.

'**Columnaris Glauca**': forms narrower, more erect columns than 'Alumii', has silver-grey foliage, and its beauty is lost as a hedge. It likes a sunny, bright or semi-shaded location, but must be protected from east winds in winter.

'**Ellwoodii**': shorter and bushier than 'Alumii', with loose columns growing to 7–10 ft (2–3 m). It also has steel-blue foliage, grey-green in summer, and its requirements are the same as 'Alumii'.

Chinese juniper
Juniperus chinensis 'Keteleeri'
Grows to 5–7 ft (1.5–2 m) — taller after 15 years — with a loosely columnar habit.

Position: sun to shade; suited to all garden soils.

Common juniper
Juniperus communis

'**Hibernica**': grows to 13–16 ft (3–4 m), with blue-grey needles.

J. c. suecica: similar to 'Hibernica', but somewhat taller.

'**Mayer**': forms columns 13–16 ft (3–4 m) tall, with loosely hanging branches and blue-grey to silvery coloured needles.

Position: sunny or well lit; otherwise not fussy.

Rocky Mountain juniper
Juniperus scopulorum 'Skyrocket'
Grows fast to form erect columns 26 ft (8 m) tall and only 2 ft (60 cm) wide.

Position: sunny or well lit.

Scots pine
Pinus sylvestris 'Fastigiata'
This columnar variety grows 13–16 ft (3–4 m) tall by 2 ft (60 cm) wide, and has steel-blue needles.

A columnar variety of juniper:
Juniperus communis *'Hibernica'*

Chamaecyparis nootkatensis *'Pendula', a variety of Nootka cypress, is among the most beautiful of all the conifers.*

Position: sunny or dappled shade; tolerates lime and dryness.

Yew
Taxus varieties

T. baccata 'Fastigiata': forms 10-ft (3-m) columns.

T. b. 'Fastigiata Aureomarginata': grows more slowly than *T. b.* 'Fastigiata', reaching only 7 ft (2 m), and has gold-edged needles that later turn light green.

T. b. 'Fastigiata Robusta': grows more erect than *T. b.* 'Fastigiata', and the needles are a lighter green.

T. b. 'Overeynderi': slower-growing and more spherical in habit, but reaching 10-16 ft (3-5 m); also suitable for hedges.

T. × media 'Hicksii': grows very slowly up to 3-5 ft (1-1.5 m), and forms loose, densely branching columns.

Position: sun to shade; lime-loving but robust.

American arbor-vitae
Thuja occidentalis 'Columna'
A narrow, densely formed columnar variety with beautiful dark green needles.

Position: sun to semi-shade.

Dwarf conifers for window boxes, troughs and smaller containers

Dwarf conifers, with their blue-green or golden yellow needles, can make very attractive tub plants even in winter. They also form an excellent backdrop for various winter and early spring flowers such as snowdrops, crocuses, early tulips, daisies and pansies.

Dwarf Hinoki cypress
Chamaecyparis obtusa 'Nana Gracilis'
Grows slowly up to 3-7 ft (1-2 m), with strangely twisted branches.

Position: well lit to semi-shaded; direct sunlight undesirable.

Dwarf Sawara cypress
Chamaecyparis pisifera varieties

'**Boulevard**': a small tree growing to 10-16 m (3-5 m), with silvery-grey foliage.

'**Filifera Nana**': a bushy shrub with ridged branches that turn downwards at the tips.

'**Golden Mop**': broader habit than 'Filifera Nana', with yellow sprays of foliage.

Position: well lit to semi-shaded; no direct sun.

Juniper
Juniperus × media varieties

'**Mint Julep**': a creeping variety with a loose growth habit, measuring 10 ft (3 m) wide by 3 ft (1 m) tall.

'**Old Gold**': slower-growing, with an even flatter growth habit, measuring 5-7 ft (1.5-2 m) wide.

Position: sun to shade; robust; suitable for any garden soil.

Flaky juniper
Juniperus squamata varieties

'**Blue Carpet**': 20 in (50 cm) tall by 5 ft (1.5 m) wide, with blue-green foliage.

'**Blue Star**': 28-35 in (70-90 cm) tall by 5 ft (1.5 m) wide, with silvery blue foliage.

Position: sun to semi-shade; robust; suitable for any garden soil.

Norway spruce
Picea abies varieties

'**Pygmaea**': a dwarf variety with a spherical habit, about 5 ft (1.5 m) tall.

'**Echiniformis**' (hedgehog spruce): a cushion-shaped form, measuring 12-20 in (30-50 cm)

tall by 30-40 in (80-100 cm) wide.

Position: sun to semi-shade; likes damp rather than dry soil, with plenty of nutrients.

White spruce
Picea glauca 'Echiniformis'
Very slow-growing, up to 12-20 in (40-50 cm) tall, with blue-green foliage.

Position: sun to semi-shade; prefers a cool, damp location.

Dwarf pines
Pinus mugo

P. m. **'Mops':** spreads to form round cushions measuring 12-16 in (30-40 cm) tall by 20-24 in (50-60 cm) wide.

P. m. pumilio: forms flat cushions across the ground measuring 20-24 in (50-60 cm) tall by 30-40 in (80-100 cm) wide.

Position: sunny or well lit; not in the shade; lime-tolerant.

Common hemlock
Tsuga canadensis 'Nana'
A dwarf variety, 12-16 in (30-40 cm) tall by 20-40 in (50-80 cm) wide, growing and spreading after 15 years.

Position: sun to semi-shade.

Conifers provide a touch of green throughout the year in the garden, in tubs or in troughs.

How to grow climbing shrubs

Climbing shrubs can transform even the smallest garden into a real paradise. Because they grow upwards they take up much less space, creating a vertical garden out of pergolas, fences, covered walkways and especially bare walls. They also provide a pleasant transition from the house to the garden, binding the two together. The house becomes part of the natural order from the first shoots of the spring, through the flowering and fruiting seasons, to the beauty of the autumn leaves — and the plants attract butterflies and songbirds throughout the year.

If climbers are trained to spread out, they can also provide effective shelter from sun, wind or rain. At the same time they can protect your buildings from the elements. Climbers trap some of the air next to the wall they're attached to, providing additional wall insulation that helps keep your house cooler in summer and warmer in winter.

With all these advantages, climbers don't need much attention, and will thrive on only a handsbreadth of soil. Many householders worry about climbers damaging the fabric of any wall or building they're attached to, and are concerned that brickwork or pebbledash may suffer. However, long experience suggests that wall surfaces don't normally suffer as long as they were sound in the first place. The one vulnerable surface seems to be modern PVC-based wall coatings; their already limited lifespan can be shortened even further by self-clinging plants such as ivy. On the other hand, climbing plants that need support shouldn't damage any wall.

It's also important to know which climbers need support in order to grow. For the most effective support, use wooden espaliers in a checkerboard or herringbone pattern. The best materials for these are pine, larch or a hardwood treated with a suitable weatherproofing medium. Alternatively you could simply use wire, threading it through loops attached to the wall, or a ready-made trellis made up of horizontal, vertical or splayed bars. Galvanised or plastic-coated wire mesh has the advantage of being less liable to rust. Whichever climbing supports you choose, fix them firmly to the wall with hooks (or dowels) and screws.

With wooden trellises or pergolas you'll have no problem tying the tendrils on securely,

*Virginia creeper (*Parthenocissus quinquefolia) *is amazingly beautiful in the autumn.*

though a nail or two can often provide extra stability. But with wire supports the shoots are liable to slip down occasionally, so it may be worth adding a climbing rope to give the young shoots a firmer support as they start to climb.

Free-standing structures like columns, pyramids, pergolas, arches and arcades can all be bought ready-made from a gardening centre. With such a wide choice there's no limit to what you can do with climbers.

Climbing shrubs can be divided into four categories according to the way they climb:

1. Tendril climbers hold on by coiling their tendrils round a suitable attachment point. They include plants such as clematis and grape vines (*Vitis*). The most suitable supports are wire meshing or espaliers.

2. Twining climbers like honeysuckle (*Lonicera*) and Russian vine (*Fallopia bald-schuanica*) hold on by coiling their stems and shoots around the support in a spiral pattern. The best supports for these plants are vertical espaliers.

3. Scrambling climbers hold on by means of long shoots, which are usually covered with thorns or prickles. They need supports with plenty of horizontal bars which they can hook or tie themselves onto. Among the best-known scramblers are climbing roses and winter jasmine (*Jasminum nudiflorum*).

4. Self-clinging climbers fasten themselves directly to a vertical surface with aerial roots or sucker-like pads. They do not usually need any further support. This group includes the ivies (*Hedera*), Virginia creeper (*Parthenocissus quinquefolia*) and Boston ivy (*P. tricuspidata*).

63

Tara vine
Actinidia arguta
A vigorously twining shrub with 16-ft (5-m) long shoots and lovely autumn colouring. Suitable for pergolas and arbours, but requires support.

Flowers: June–July, clusters of fragrant white flowers hidden among the foliage.

Fruits: edible berries with a high vitamin C content.

Position: sunny and warm.

Care: only cut back young shoots.

Dutchman's pipe
Aristolochia durior
A vigorously growing, self-clinging climber with 20–33-ft (6–10-m) long shoots. Suitable for pergolas, tree trunks and house walls. Some wire may be helpful in providing support.

Flowers: June–August, pipe-shaped, up to 12 in (30 cm) long, yellowish-green with red-brown veins, and purplish-brown inside.

Position: sunny to shaded, damp.

Care: tolerates even drastic pruning.

Trumpet vine
Campsis radicans and *C.* 'Madame Galen'
Climbs to 23–30 ft (7–9 m) by means of aerial roots. Suitable for walls, pergolas and tree trunks. 'Madame Galen' has large, prettily shaped pinnate leaves measuring some 16 in (40 cm).

Flowers: August–September; orange-red on *C. radicans*, bigger and salmon-red on 'Madame Galen'.

Position: sunny and warm, but roots need shade (use a ground-cover plant).

Care: prune back in the late summer; provide some support after planting.

Staff vine
Celastrus orbiculatus
Will grow to 33 ft (10 m) on a pergola, but will strangle a tree. Leaves turn yellow in the autumn.

Flowers: insignificant.

This gorgeous large-flowered clematis looks really good on a rose arch.

Fruits: beautiful, yellow and scarlet, but poisonous.

Position: sunny to shaded, undemanding.

Care: prune as necessary.

Large-flowered clematis
Clematis hybrids
Climbing plants with gorgeous flowers ranging in colour from white, through blue, pink, red and violet to pink and red striped, depending on the variety. Growth height also varies according to variety, ranging from 7 ft (2 m) to 13 ft (4 m). Clematis will flower on pergolas, espaliers or wire supports.

Flowers: the season varies according to variety, ranging from May–June ('Lasurstern', lavender blue) to August–October ('Lady Betty Balfour', deep purple).

Position: the upper parts of the shoots tolerate sun as well as semi-shade. Even so, don't plant on a south-facing wall as this will be too dry, and avoid any dripping water (e.g. from a leaking gutter). Keep the roots cool and damp by planting ground cover (e.g. ivy or cotoneaster) or using stones for shade.

Planting: dig out a trench two spades deep, and fill it with a mixture of leaf mould, compost, alkaline fertiliser (no peat!) and nutritious garden soil; plant deep, so the tops of the roots are 2–4 in (5–10 cm) below the soil and don't get dry.

Care: plants that flower in the summer on one-year-old shoots should be pruned back to 2 ft (60 cm) in the early spring. These summer-flowering forms include *C. × jackmanii*, 'Gipsy Queen', 'Nelly Moser', 'Ernest Markham', 'Lady Betty Balfour' and 'Ville de Lyon'. As for late spring flowerers such as 'Lasurstern', 'Madame Le Coultre', 'Rouge Cardinal' and *C. montana rubens* (see below), just thin them a little in February or March, and remove the seed heads. Any more pruning will mean fewer flowers.

Montana clematis
C. montana
A fast-growing climber (16–26 ft; 5–8 m) that's covered in flowers from April to June. The pretty, small to medium-sized blooms vary in colour between *C. m. rubens* (pink), 'Superba' (white) and 'Tetrarose' (lilac-pink).

Position/care: as for the spring-flowering hybrids (see above).

The popular clematis is available in innumerable varieties, with flowers in a whole range of colours and shapes.

Other clematis species
In most of these plants the flowers are only small, but cluster together to form glorious inflorescences, ideal for gardeners who like unusual but natural-looking plants.

Alpine clematis (*C. alpina*): climbs to only 7 ft (2 m), and bears blue and white flowers in April and May, followed by feathery seedheads. Requires the same position as the hybrids, but not fussy about soil. Drastic pruning possible before growth begins.

C. indivisa: climbs to 16 ft (5 m), with large, fragrant white flowers from September to October. For climbing frames and walls. Requires the same position as the hybrids. Prune down to 2 ft (60 cm) before

The yellow blooms of Clematis tangutica *are among the most delightful of flowers.*

growth begins. Needs shelter, and a warm autumn for good flowering.

***C. tangutica*:** climbs to 10 ft (3 m), with bell-shaped yellow flowers from June into the autumn. Long-flowering, with silvery-coloured seedheads to follow. Requires the same position and care as the hybrids.

Old man's beard or Traveller's Joy (*C. vitalba*): climbs to 26 ft (8 m) and bears slightly fragrant white flowers from July to

October. Long-flowering, with silvery-coloured seedheads lasting through winter. Looks good when climbing on older trees or dark-coloured conifers. Requires the same position as the hybrids, but is not fussy about soil. Can be pruned to 2 ft (60 cm) before growth begins.

***C. viticella*:** climbs to about 10–13 ft (3–4 m), with beautiful violet-red flowers from June to August and silvery-coloured seedheads. Suitable as an espalier or for pergolas and trellises. Requires the same position as the hybrids, but is not fussy about soil. Can be pruned to 2 ft (60 cm) before growth begins.

English ivy
Hedera helix
Climbs to over 33 ft (10 m) by means of aerial roots, or spreads as ground cover (8 in; 20 cm). This evergreen plant is suitable for north-facing walls or old trees.

***H. h.* 'Oro di Bogliasco'** is particularly attractive, with its somewhat smaller, golden-centred leaves.

Flowers: first flowers appear after 10 years.

Fruits: small, blue-black and spherical, following the flowers in spring.

Position: sunny to shaded; humus-rich soil, not too poor in nutrients.

Care: prune as much as you like.

Irish ivy
Hedera hibernica
Similar in most respects to English ivy, but faster-growing, with large leaves and insignificant fruits.

Position/care: same as for English ivy.

Climbing hydrangea
Hydrangea anomala petiolaris
A magnificent climbing shrub with reddish-brown shoots. It is self-clinging and grows to 33 ft (10 m). Suitable for walls and pergolas.

Flowers: June–July, large, loosely structured white flower heads.

Position: semi-shade to shade; damp, sandy, nutritious soil.

Care: prune after the winter so that the flowers grow larger; drastic pruning possible.

Winter jasmine
Jasminum nudiflorum
A scrambling shrub that climbs to 7 ft (2 m). The slender green shoots need to be tied to a trellis, though it will also hang down from the top of a wall, or it can be planted between leafless shrubs that will provide anchorage.

Flowers: yellow, like primulas; often appear as early as November and continue until March.

Position: lime-loving, undemanding, tolerates poor soils.

Care: thin out if the branches become overcrowded; will tolerate drastic pruning.

Goatleaf honeysuckle
Lonicera caprifolium
A vigorous climber, growing to 10–16 ft (3–5 m), suitable for pergolas, fences and bare trees.

Flowers: May–June; a profusion of yellowish-white flowers, reddish on the outside.

Fruits: coral-red berries, highly poisonous.

Position: likes damp, lime-rich soil in a shaded location.

Climbing honeysuckles (Lonicera) can be trained to form a highly decorative arch.

Care: renovation pruning recommended.

Scarlet trumpet honeysuckle
L. 'Dropmore Scarlet'
A vigorous twining shrub, growing to 10 ft (3 m), and suitable for pergolas, patios and the tops of walls.

Flowers: long-flowering from June through to autumn; red flowers.

Fruits: poisonous berries.

Position: sunny; likes damp soi;, otherwise undemanding.

Care: thin out the shoots if they become overcrowded.

Gold flame honeysuckle
Lonicera × heckrottii

A lovely twining shrub growing to 10-13 ft (3-4 m), suitable for pergolas, trellises and fences.

Flowers/fruits: long-flowering June–autumn; red, later yellow and red. Poisonous berries.

Position/care: as for scarlet trumpet honeysuckle.

Above Lonicera × heckrottii *is a twining honeysuckle of great beauty.*

Right *No garden should be without Chinese wisteria (*Wisteria sinensis*).*

Evergreen honeysuckle
L. henryi

An evergreen twining shrub that grows to 16 ft (5 m) and will climb on pergolas, trellises and even old trees.

Flowers: June–August; insignificant, yellow to red.

Fruits: poisonous black berries.

Position: sun to shade; nutritious soil.

Care: prune or thin out as necessary.

Lonicera × tellmanniana

A handsome, vigorously twining shrub that will grow to 16 ft (5 m) on a trellis or pergola.

Flowers: June–July; masses of fragrant orange-yellow flowers.

Fruits: light red berries, poisonous.

Position: sunny, nutritious soil.

Care: prune or thin as needed

Virginia creeper
Parthenocissus quinquefolia

A self-clinging shrub that climbs to 33 ft (10 m). Its leaves turn bright scarlet in the autumn.

P. q. engelmannii has a more decorative leaf pattern than the species, but insignificant fruits and flowers.

Position: sun to semi-shade; undemanding.

Care: prune as much as you like.

Boston ivy
P. tricuspidata 'Veitchii'

Similar to Virginia creeper, but grows particularly fast. Sucker-like pads help it cling tightly to walls. Foliage turns orange-yellow or scarlet in autumn.

Position/care: as for Virginia creeper.

Russian vine, mile-a-minute plant
Fallopia baldschuanica

A twining shrub that climbs to 33 ft (10 m); very fast-growing, often proliferating out of control. Covers walls, pergolas, arcades and large trees with a coat of green.

Flowers: July–October; large white flower panicles.

Position: sun to semi-shade; totally undemanding.

Care: annual pruning recommended; needs climbing support.

Chinese wisteria
Wisteria sinensis

A magnificent, vigorously growing shrub with rope-like shoots that grow up to 33 ft (10 m) long. Looks particularly good on a house wall or pergola, but needs a trellis or wire for support. **NB: all parts of this plant are poisonous.**

Flowers: April–May, in 12-in (30-cm) long, violet clusters.

Position: likes a sunny, well-sheltered location, with nutritious soil that should never be allowed to go dry.

Care: many wisterias take years to come into flower, but if a plant persistently refuses to flower, it may be a non-flowering seedling and you should simply dig it up. Make sure to prune back the side shoots from the current year (immediately after flowering if possible).

Producing the perfect hedge

If you want to mark the boundaries of your garden, what better way to do it than with a wall of living plants? A hedge offers privacy, and shelters the garden from the noise and dust of the street outside. In windy locations it will improve the microclimate, allowing you to stay out in the garden much longer in the evenings. Hedges of hornbeam, privet or field maple give excellent protection against cold northerly or easterly winds.

Some hedges provide good nesting sites for many species of songbird, which like to take advantage of the shelter they provide. This is another factor that may influence your choice of hedging plant.

To produce a good hedge, it's essential that the plant you choose should respond to continual pruning by producing denser growth. You're aiming for a finished hedge that's about three times taller than its depth from front to back. As a rule of thumb, the depth of your hedge should be 10 in (25 cm) at the very least, but while a hornbeam hedge can be relatively narrow, a hawthorn or privet hedge needs to be about 12-14 in (30-35 cm) deep. Other plants such as field maple, cornelian cherry or holly need as much depth or even a little more. Hedges of arbor-vitae (*Thuja*) or false cypress

(*Chamaecyparis*) need even more space, and if you want a spruce hedge you should allow at least 3 ft (1 m).

Planting

When planting a hedge it's particularly important to prepare the soil properly before you start. If you want to do a really thorough job, dig out a trench for the hedge at least 3 ft (1 m) from the garden boundary and fill it with a loose planting compost that contains plenty of nutrients. For instance, you could use some good homemade garden compost mixed with blood-fish-and-bone or bonemeal. If you already have really good soil, then you can make the job a little simpler: just dig over two spadefuls of soil for each plant, spread a layer of that same planting mixture on top, and gently rake it in. Before you actually start planting, it's best to leave the prepared soil for about a week, keeping it moist all the time.

Prepare the plant roots immediately before planting. If they're in a container, remove it. If the root ball is wrapped in cloth netting, cut the knots holding it on. If the roots are bare, cut them back a little (see page 80

A hedge helps protect the garden from all the noise and dust of the street — it also gives you a little privacy.

for more detailed instructions). Now put the plants in, close enough together so that they just touch. In most cases one row of plants is enough, but two for hornbeam or privet we'd recommend two rows. It's

A high hedge can be made less forbidding by having an ornamental planted in front of it. Here × Cupressocyparis leylandii 'Castlewellan Gold' is offset by Hedera colchica 'Dentata Variegata'.

also a good idea to lay a length of string as a guide to ensure a regular line.

It's best to have two people in your planting team. One holds the plant firmly, moving it gently to and fro to make sure the soil beds in close to the roots, while the other fills in the soil around the roots. Finally, stamp the soil down firmly around the plant, and give it a good watering before moving on to the next.

How many plants per metre?

The number of plants you'll need for each yard (metre) of hedge will vary according to the species or variety. Here's a list of some of the commonest broadleaf hedge species:

Field maple (*Acer campestre*): 3-5 plants per yard (metre).
Hedge barberry (*Berberis thunbergii*): 3-5 plants.
Common hornbeam (*Carpinus betulus*): 3-5 plants.

Japanese quince (*Chaenomeles japonica*): 4–7 plants.

Cornelian cherry (*Cornus mas*): 3–5 plants.

Common hawthorn (*Crataegus monogyna*): 3–5 plants.

Common beech (*Fagus silvatica*): 3–5 plants.

Privet (*Ligustrum* species): 4–5 plants.

Oregon grape (*Mahonia aquifolium*): 4–5 plants.

Shrubby cinquefoil (*Potentilla fruticosa*): 4–5 plants (formal cutting recommended).

Firethorn (*Pyracantha coccinea*): 5–6 plants.

Alpine currant (*Ribes alpinum* 'Schmidt'): 3–5 plants.

Spiraea (*Spiraea × vanhouttei*): 3–5 plants.

Informal flower hedges

If you have the space for it, you could opt for a more informal flowering hedge instead of a severely clipped green hedge. The plants will still need a little pruning, but they can be allowed to retain their natural shape. For flowering hedges, 2–3 plants per yard (metre) will be enough.

Before planting this kind of hedge, you should check with your next-door neighbours that they don't object to flowering shrubs along their garden borders. Since you can't take their permission for granted, a flowering hedge may often be more appropriate for an outside boundary bordering the street, or around a patio or any other free space within the garden.

Coniferous hedges

Coniferous shrubs, with their heavily branching growth habit, make ideal hedges for songbirds to nest in. This is especially true of the arbor-vitae (*Thuja*), which can be allowed to grow as high as 7 ft (2 m). Apart from the 'natural' forms, there are species and varieties with a bushier habit that will also work very well. We recommend using about 2–3 plants per yard (metre). Conifers can be pruned in exactly the same way as the deciduous hedge species, but at a different time.

Our native yews (*Taxus* species) are noted for their compact growth habit and dark

This mixed hedge combines spiraea, forsythia and purple barberry, replacing the usual green with a medley of colours.

green needles. They make good hedge plants because they are tolerant of shade, and you won't spoil their appearance by heavy pruning. They spread out so well that two plants per yard (metre) are quite enough.

Spruce (*Picea*) is good for tall-growing hedges, but it does need a lot of moisture, even in winter. Just two plants per yard (metre) are required here.

The columnar false cypresses (*Chamaecyparis* varieties) will grow together to form a dense and very colourful border hedge, especially if you combine different varieties with blue, green or yellow sprays of foliage. You can take a pair of shears to them if you want to, but if you do, much of their beauty will be lost.

Columnar junipers (*Juniperus* varieties) will form an even narrower hedge than the false cypresses. Plant about three of these per yard (metre), but not necessarily in a straight line — a slightly zigzag pattern will look less severe.

Feeding

Because hedge plants grow so closely together in a small area, they make heavy demands on the nutrients in the soil. To compensate for this you should fertilise them regularly at least once a year (beginning in the year of planting). Cover the soil around each plant with a good layer of garden compost (or well-rotted animal manure).

Put down some additional fertiliser just before the spring growth begins. Use about 2–3 oz/yd (60–90 g/m) of an organic fertiliser such as blood-fish-and-bone, raking it gently into the soil after application.

Pruning

Newly planted hedges

When you've planted your hedge, don't be afraid to cut back both leading and side shoots by at least a third, and preferably by as much as two-

To stop a pine growing too tall, halve the length of the main shoots.

thirds. This will encourage the young plants to branch heavily, producing a dense, impenetrable mass of branches and shoots starting close to the ground — the mark of a really good hedge. Experts will even cut back young privet, hawthorn or cornelian cherry hedges by the same amount just one year after planting — and such drastic treatment is always desirable if your original plants were short of side shoots.

Mature hedges

Evergreen hedges need pruning only once a year (late in the summer). Deciduous hedges (e.g. hornbeam, beech, privet or hawthorn) need to be pruned

once or twice a year. Some, such as *Lonicera nitida*, need clipping every six weeks.

The main summer clipping is to keep the hedge generally tidy and attractive. It shouldn't be necessary until the hedge starts to look unkempt, but wait until July if you can so as not to disturb any songbirds that have nested among the branches. If you're a stickler for tidiness, though, you might prefer to trim your hedge twice during the growth period — once in May when the year's growth is only half complete, and again at the height of the summer. Alternatively, the first trim can be early in August, with a second in mid-September if there's been some secondary growth.

Deciduous hedges sometimes need formative pruning between October and March, when they're dormant. This will ensure the hedge acquires (or retains) its proper shape. To control its height and depth and achieve the effect you want, you may have to cut back into wood that's already several years old.

Ideally, a hedge should have a symmetrical cross-section, but the sides should be steeply angled rather than vertical. The base of the hedge needs to be wider than the top — about one-fifth wider, to be precise. If the sides of the hedge are vertical, its lower branches will receive little or no light, and they'll gradually die off. With privet hedges you can round off the top edges to give a softer effect. Generally speaking, it's much easier to shape a hedge if it isn't allowed to grow too tall.

These rules mainly apply to formal clipped hedges, but they do have some relevance for more informal, free-growing hedges when they are used to mark garden boundaries. Here, though, you'll normally need your shears only if you want to tidy a bush that has got out of hand, or to cut a small branch covered with flowers or berries for display in a vase. Treatment may occasionally be necessary if branches start to get overcrowded, if the hedge grows too high, or if one of the main stems grows out too much and creates an unbalanced effect.

As a rule, the tiny hedges used for edging flower beds will need pruning only once a year, and that should be in spring. Some may need more frequent pruning, e.g. low-growing Japanese spiraeas (*Spiraea japonica* 'Little Princess'), dwarf evergreen honeysuckle (*Lonicera nitida* 'Elegant') and dwarf box (*Buxus sempervirens* 'Suffruticosa').

Renovating an old hedge
If an old hedge has become really bare and ugly, renovation pruning is the only solution. The treatment is invariably drastic: you'll have to cut (or even saw) the main stems to within 10 in (25 cm) of the ground. This is done in winter, and applies only to deciduous hedges, never to evergreens.

The best pruning shears have two blades and a proper safety catch.

Evergreen hedges
Evergreen hedges, whether broad-leaved or coniferous, shouldn't be treated in the same way as their deciduous counterparts. Prune them just once a year, preferably before growth begins in the spring — or better yet, in the early autumn, from August to the beginning of September. Never leave pruning until the late spring, because this will stop the new year's growth in its tracks.

If you're a stickler for tidiness, you might want to prune your hedges twice a year, and you'll certainly need to do some extra trimming if you want to reproduce those attractive geometrical or animal figures so often seen around large country estates. But whatever you're trying to do, make sure that the leafy shoots from the previous year are always left intact; you should simply shorten the current year's growth.

With coniferous hedges, as with broadleaves, it's advisable to trim the sides at an angle so the hedge is wider at the base than it is at the top. That way, a few bare brown branches won't be very obvious even if you can see them.

Laying out a front garden with shrubs

If you want to lay out or restore a front garden, there are a few points you should always bear in mind. Firstly, don't just plant any old how. Different plants grow best in different positions, and your choice of what to plant where should take account of the microclimate and the prevailing soil and light conditions in your garden. Sun-loving plants won't grow in the shade, for example, while shade-loving plants don't need any sun, and probably won't like it, either.

Secondly, all plants need enough space around them to develop properly. If you plant them too close together, your garden won't look as good as it could do. More importantly, your plants will become disease-ridden and they'll have to be pruned far more severely than is normally good for them.

Never plant large trees in your front garden, and never use low-growing shrubs that spread out more than 13–20 ft (4–6 m). Free-growing hedges need a space of at least 10 ft (3 m), while formal hedges need no more than 2–4 ft (60–120 cm). Climbing shrubs are even less space-hungry: they'll be happy with just 20 in (50 cm).

Some sample layouts

For a detached suburban house

This garden is in a very shady location on the north side of the

house, where the pine (*Pinus*) provides a visual focus. The shrubs include a number of beautiful species and varieties of rhododendron or azalea (*Rhododendron*) that flower from early April until the end of June.

The flowering dogwood (*Cornus kousa*) produces some gorgeous blossoms. The velvet hydrangea (*Hydrangea aspera sargentiana*) is a feast for the eyes with its downy leaves and white-edged flower clusters, and much the same applies to the climbing hydrangea (*H. anomala petiolaris*).

Growing around the base of the shrubs are plantain lilies

(*Hosta*), the fern *Dryopteris affinis*, creeping variegated strawberries (*Duchesnea indica* 'Harlequin') and foam flowers (*Tiarella cordifolia*).

76

From left to right:
Rhododendron cataw-
biense *and* R. yakushim-
anum *hybrids (white),* R. wardii
*(yellow) with flowering dogwood
(*Cornus kousa*) behind, a Scots pine
(*Pinus sylvestris*) above with azaleas (*Rhododendron*) in front of it, and on the far right a
velvet hydrangea (*Hydrangea aspera sargentiana*) and a climbing hydrangea (*H. anomala
petiolaris*) growing up into the pine.*

For a semi-detached house in a quiet suburb (below)

This garden is in a semi-shaded position to the east of the house. A sturdy field maple (*Acer campestre*) and a rowan (*Sorbus aucuparia*) help to give the garden a feeling of size. *Viburnum* species such as the evergreen *V. rhytodiphyllum*, the semi-evergreen *V. × burk-woodii*, and the winter-flowering *V. farreri* make this a highly attractive garden. *Corylopsis spicata* is one of the finest flowering shrubs, as is the *Stranvaesia* shown on the left-hand edge of the picture with its hoards of red berries. Evergreen shrubs include *Mahonia*, dwarf box (*Buxus*) and ivy (*Hedera*).

Among the perennials growing in this garden are meadow cranesbill (*Geranium pratense*), red avens (*Geum coccineum*), Japanese anemone (*Anemone × hybrida*), Rose of Sharon (*Hypericum calycinum*) and alpine forget-me-not (*Myosotis alpestris*).

The list is endless, proving that there are trees or shrubs suited to every situation or position in a garden.

For a terraced house in a town (right)

This west-facing garden is only occasionally in the sun, and is best suited to sturdier plants. In the middle is a pink-flowered hawthorn (*Crataegus*), which should preferably have a broad crown. Montana clematis (*Clematis montana rubens*) makes a good wall plant, and an upright-growing box hedge (*Buxus*) helps to keep the garden private.

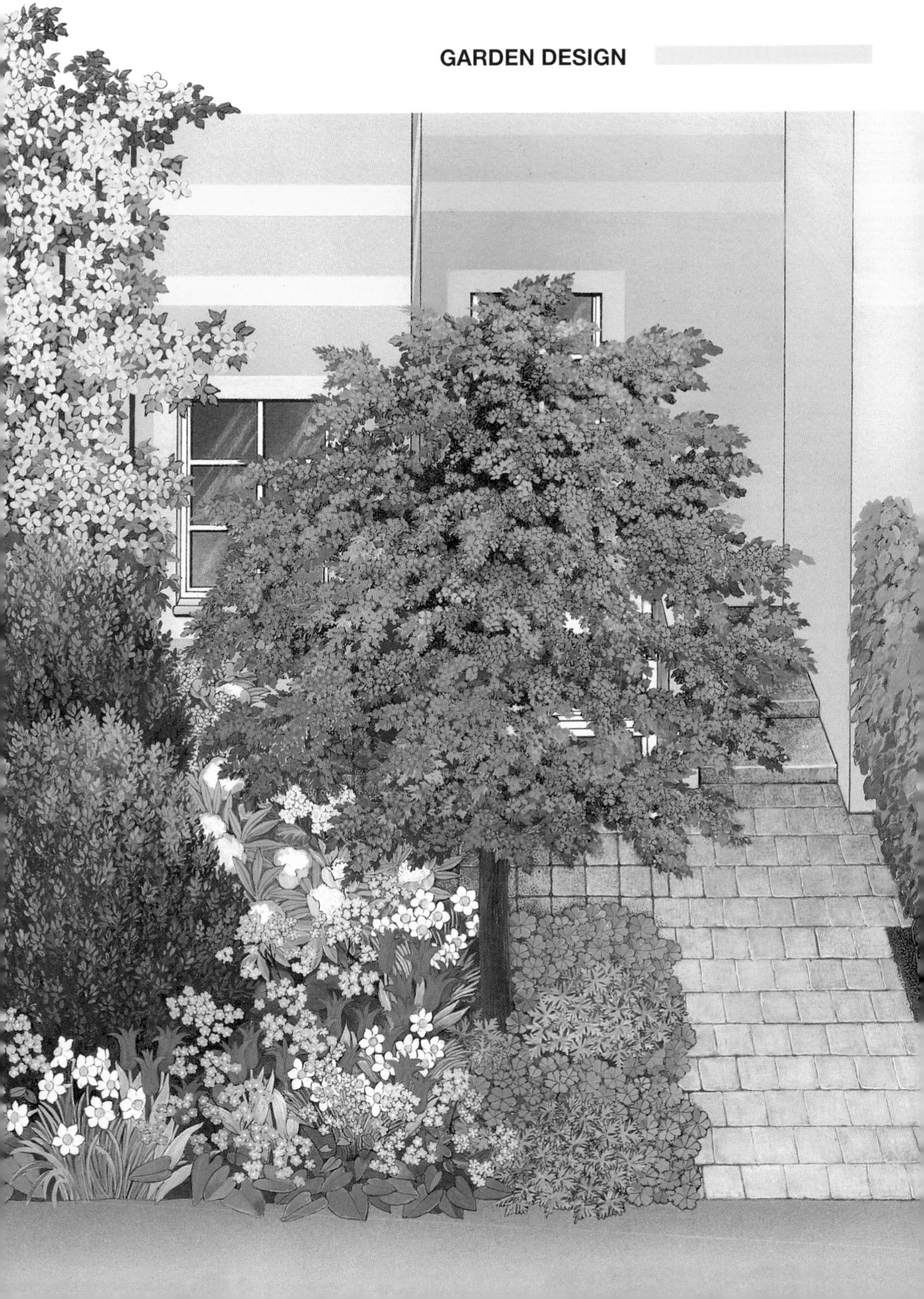

Preparation and planting

In many gardens you'll find the soil has become compacted. This is particularly likely with heavy clay soils, or in the gardens of newly built houses. Plants always do badly in these conditions, because the soil is too compressed to allow an effective exchange of water between the soil surface and the underlying water table. In wet weather the roots become waterlogged, which makes them rot, and in prolonged dry weather they will dry out completely.

The quality of your plants rarely has much to do with growth problems or poor flowering. The more usual reason is poor soil preparation before the affected shrubs were planted. All trees and shrubs need to be planted in a light, loosely structured soil with plenty of humus.

Humus can easily be added to soil. It's produced by rotting down various organic materials such as leaves, lawn clippings, animal manure, chopped-up twigs and bark mulch. You should cover the ground with some of these every year in a process known as mulching. Without the regular addition of these humus-forming materials, your shrubs will soon become reluctant to grow or flower. Before mulching, loosen up the soil and add some organic fertiliser (see page 85).

Never try to improve the soil just by adding large amounts of fertiliser. It is also inadvisable to fill the planting hole with soil mixed with pre-fertilised peat products. These can be extremely effective in the short term, but they tend to spoil the plant. Later on it will have problems putting roots out into the surrounding soils, because they are heavier, and also poorer in humus and essential nutrients. The eventual result will be weak shoots and floppy branches. You'll get the best results by adding crumbled or half-rotted compost to the soil before putting it back around the plant.

Mix the soil you have removed from the planting hole with a few handfuls of organic fertiliser (e.g. granulated farm manure, hoof-and-hornmeal or bonemeal). After you've put it back, rake some bark mulch into the upper soil layers, but don't dig this in.

If you want your plants to grow well and stay healthy, make sure you prepare the soil properly before planting.

Above *Shrubs can be sold in one of three ways: with bare roots, with the root ball wrapped in cloth netting, or with the roots in a container.*

Right *Cut out any damaged roots before planting.*

In the case of conifers or evergreen broad-leaved shrubs, the planting hole should be just deep enough to contain the full height of the root ball. For deciduous trees or shrubs it's best to add an extra 4 in (20 cm). The planting hole should be twice as wide as the roots.

When you're planting a root-balled tree, remember to cut open the knots in the covering netting, but don't actually take it off. Only pots or plastic bags should be removed for planting. If you're planting a bare-rooted shrub, cut off any broken or damaged roots; if any of the roots are too long, cut them back to about half their length.

Put the plant in the hole so it's at the same depth it was in the nursery where it came from. This is easy to check by looking at the soil mark on the stem. Never plant a shrub any higher or lower in the soil than this. The result could be disastrous (with rhododendrons, in partic-ular); the very few exceptions (e.g. tree peonies and clematis) only go to prove the rule.

Wiggle the plant vigorously as you replace the soil. This ensures that the soil is well distributed around the roots, and stops you planting the shrub too deep. Finally, use your feet to press the soil down around the plant, forming a slight depression into which water will drain.

You'll need to stake trees or standard shrubs. If you don't, they may easily fall over in the wind, which puts a severe strain on the roots. It's best to set up the stake first and then put the plant in next to it.

Planting conifers

Conifers are usually sold either in containers or with their root balls wrapped in cloth netting. Both methods have the advan-tage that you don't have to plant immediately. On the other hand, you can plant conifers at any time of year except in severe frost.

Before you plant shrubs next to a house, make sure they'll get enough water. One way of doing this is to raise the level of the adjoining ground with turf or stones: this will encourage water to drain down onto the plants.

If your conifer comes with a root ball, put the plant in the hole you've prepared for it, then cut open the netting and pull it out carefully from under the root ball. If the plant's in a container, remove the roots from the container, scratch open the soil surface of the root ball a little, and put the roots in the planting hole. Now fill in the soil, press it down firmly, and water thoroughly until it begins to subside and the water is no longer being absorbed. Use any remaining soil to create a rim that will encourage water to drain in towards the plant.

It's better for any larger plant to be staked. Put the stake on the side of the plant facing the prevailing wind. When you're tying the plant to the stake, never put any wire in direct contact with the stem or trunk — use a pair of nylon tights, a piece of bicycle tyre or a propri-etary tree tie, which won't damage the plant.

Transplanting a tree

Before moving an older plant you should decide whether the job is really worth doing, or whether you might do better to plant a new tree or shrub instead. You'll get a lot of pleasure from watching a young magnolia or Japanese maple as it grows and develops, and the plant will be less liable to growth problems.

If you do decide to transplant an older, larger tree, then do the job while it's dormant. Use a spade to cut out a substantial root ball, and cover this with wire netting or hessian. Now lift the plant out carefully and move it to its new location. Replant the tree at exactly the same depth as it was previously.

Afterwards, prune back the crown of the tree by about 20-30 per cent, and give the plant a really good watering. As always, good, regular watering should ensure that the plant continues to flourish in its new position.

If you bought your plant with its root ball wrapped in sacking, cut open the sacking as you plant it.

Watering, mulching and feeding

Watering

Newly planted trees and shrubs need regular watering just as much as older, more mature plants. This is particularly important if there's been no rain for several weeks, or if the soil is extremely light and doesn't retain moisture very well. Hedges need large quantities of water, because the plants are growing close together and very little water gets into the surrounding soil. You may need to put out a garden hose and let it run for an hour or so.

With solitary trees or shrubs, it's best to make a depression around the plant so the water can flow down into it: this will stop the water going to waste. This depression should be as wide as the base of the tree canopy (the drip line).

> If the summer's been dry, give all your evergreen plants a thorough watering in the autumn so they're not dry as they go into the winter.

If daily watering gets no further than the surface of the soil it is effectively useless. It may even be damaging, because it will turn the surface soil to mud.

Mulching

Mulching involves covering the soil with organic materials such as rotted garden compost, leaf mould, grass cuttings, chopped-up branches and twigs, or bark mulch. The layer of mulch should never be more than 2-3 in (6-8 cm) thick. Mulching is an extremely beneficial process. It stops the soil from drying out in the wind or sun, and it also gives protection from frost. More than that, it provides food for worms and other soil life, which then turn it into humus.

Regular mulching usually prevents any problem with weeds, but if you need to do any hoeing, be careful to turn over just the surface of the soil, leaving the roots untouched. Never dig the soil between shrubs, as this is a good way to destroy vital root systems.

Feeding

All shrubs, especially hedge plants, need a well-balanced supply of nutrients: nitrogen (N) for leaf development, phosphorus (P) for flower formation, and potassium (K) to help ripen and stabilise the woody shoots. Apart from that, various trace elements are also essential.

Ornamental trees and shrubs thrive best in a loosely struc-

Apply powdered or granular fertiliser as early as possible in the year, preferably in February or March.

tured, humus-rich soil. The best way of getting this is to apply regular doses of rotted garden compost, or well-rotted manure with plenty of straw in it. Alternatively, garden centres offer bags of ready-made organic compost, and you can also buy dried or composted farm manures of various kinds. In the late autumn put down a 2–4-in (5–10-cm) layer of these nutri-

tious materials to activate the soil life and encourage the formation of humus. Spread it around the drip line of trees and on the soil surrounding your shrubs.

This is also the time to apply various organic fertilisers such as bonemeal, hoof-and-horn-meal, blood-fish-and-bone or granulated farm manures, since these often take several months to become active in the soil. On the other hand, fast-working inorganic compounds should be applied in late winter or early spring — February or March to be more specific. The plant starts to absorb nutrients before the spring growth begins, and the absorption rate is especially high just after that, so it's important to time the feeding correctly.

The summer feed should take place in June, just as the seed heads are developing on the spring-flowering plants. Don't feed your shrubs any later, as this will extend the growth period, and the wood won't ripen or harden up enough to withstand the first frosts.

Hedge plants also need regular feeding; it's best to use a liquid manure. When your hedge has grown to the height you want, halve the amount of fertiliser that you apply.

Suitable fertilisers

There's a wide range of fertilisers on the market. The following are just some of those that would be suitable for use on shrubs, trees and climbers: Growmore, a general, balanced fertiliser containing N, P and K in the ratio 7:7:7; Miracle-gro (ICI) and Miracid (ICI), good for rhodo-dendrons and other lime-hating plants; Phostrogen (9:10:26), good for flowering shrubs, also contains trace elements; blood-fish-and-bone, a bulky, slow-acting organic fertiliser that lasts all season; Bio Friendly plant food (PBI, 7:5:5), contains both organic and mineral nutrients; bonemeal (mainly P with a little N), good at planting time; hoof-and-hornmeal (mainly N), slow-acting; Maxicrop, seaweed-based, containing many trace elements; Maxicrop + Sequester-ed Iron for acid-soil plants; Bio Plant Food (PBI), seaweed-based (5:5:6) with added nutrients.

There are also specialist rose fertilisers, and soil conditioners/fertilisers such as Lady Muck and 6X which are specially treated, concentrated farm manures. Some are in pellet or powder form, and should be applied once or twice a season. Others are liquid, and are watered on once a week or fortnightly according to the makers' instructions.

If you prefer inorganic fertilisers, make sure they don't contain chlorides and are rich in both potassium and phospho-rus; they should also contain trace elements.

Pruning

Nearly all ornamental shrubs need regular pruning to keep their shape and size, and to prevent them crowding out other plants. If you prune them correctly at regular intervals, with a suitable pair of secateurs, they will thrive, and they'll also be less vulnerable to pests and diseases. If a tree or bush has an open, loosely branching crown, there will be too much air and light inside the plant for pests or fungal diseases to survive.

It's true that many ornamental shrubs will grow into vigorous plants without pruning, but even these will only be encouraged to flower really vigorously if you shorten their twigs and branches to the right length. The older parts of a shrub will gradually die off anyway, while the rootstock will continually put out new shoots. So at the very least you should remove all the dead wood, plus any branches that are crossed over or rubbing against each other.

At the same time, always remember that every tree and shrub is different; the worst thing you can do is to treat them all the same way. Always adjust your pruning methods carefully to take account of each plant's natural growth habit and flowering season.

With clever pruning you can turn a privet or box hedge into a series of decorative arches or animal shapes.

Summer-flowering shrubs

All summer-flowering shrubs and trees like a vigorous pruning early in the year, preferably in March or early April when the sap is rising. They can also be pruned in late summer or autumn, immediately after flowering, but this isn't advisable in cold gardens. Keep the strong shoots, but trim them down to 4–12 in (10–30 cm) so that only a few nodes are left. Cut out weak twigs or branches altogether. The following plants should be pruned in this way:

butterfly bush (*Buddleia davidii*)
summer-flowering spiraeas (*Spiraea japonica albiflora*, 'Anthony Waterer', *S. decumbens*, 'Froebelii', 'Little Princess' and *S. douglasii*)

the deciduous *Ceanothus*
dyer's greenweed (*Genista
tinctoria*)
winter-hardy forms of the
shrubby hibiscus (*Hibiscus
syriacus*)
Hydrangea paniculata
'Grandiflora'.

Spring-flowering shrubs

Spring-flowering shrubs
shouldn't be pruned in the late
winter or early spring, because
the flower buds will already be

forming. Wait until they've
finished flowering. Even then
you should normally only
remove older, flowered twigs
and branches. If you don't
prune these then the new,
young shoots, whose flower
buds are already forming ready
to flower next spring, won't
develop properly.

If, on the other hand, a shrub
has grown too big and is reluctant to flower, then prune it
back drastically, removing all the
older wood. This is easy to
recognise from the darker
colour of the bark.

The following plants should be
pruned immediately after
flowering:

cornelian cherry (*Cornus mas*)
forsythias
dwarf almonds (*Prunus triloba*
and *P. tenella*)
ornamental plums (*Prunus ×
blireana* and *P. cerasifera*)
spring-flowering spiraeas
deciduous viburnums
(*Viburnum farreri*, *V.
lantana*, *V. opulus* 'Roseum',
V. plicatum 'Maresii', and *V. p.
f. tomentosum*)
common broom (*Cytisus
scoparius*)
Warminster broom (*C. × praecox* varieties)
flowering currant (*Ribes
sanguineum*).

The following are pruned in
summer as soon as flowering
has finished:

deutzias
weigelas
lilacs (*Syringa*)

golden rose of China (*Rosa
xanthina hugonis*)
centifolia roses (*R. × centifolia*
varieties)
once-flowering climbing roses.

Pruning climbing shrubs

Climbing shrubs should mostly
be spared any regular or drastic
pruning. Don't reach for your
secateurs unless they've really
grown into a tangle. This often
happens, for example, with
Russian vine (*Fallopia bald-
schuanica*) or honeysuckle
(*Lonicera*). Neither of these
plants forms proper stems
anyway, and you can happily cut
them right back; the long shoots
will grow back very quickly. If
the lower parts of the plant
have become ugly and bare, you
can even prune them to within
inches of the ground.

With self-clinging climbers
such as ivy (*Hedera*) and Virginia creeper (*Parthenocissus*),
you just need to cut off the tip
and side shoots to stop them
proliferating. More vigorous
pruning is also possible, and
with ivy it may actually be
necessary, as it becomes too
heavy after only a few years.

Some plants such as Chinese
wisteria (*Wisteria sinensis*) and
staff vine (*Celastrus*) will only
flower on older wood. With the
staff vine, simply remove the
tips. Wisteria is pruned differ-
ently: in July, cut the new side
shoots back to about 6 in (15
cm), and then in winter cut
back to one bud. This increases
flowering and keeps the plant

87

within bounds. If you want more growth, you can omit the winter pruning.

Different clematis varieties need different treatments. Spring-flowering clematis should only be thinned a little in the spring, retaining the vigorously growing older wood. Summer-flowering varieties can stand much more drastic treatment, and you can even cut into the older wood.

The latter group comprises most varieties of large-flowered clematis: these should be pruned fairly hard in early spring, to leave about 2 ft (60 cm) of stem above ground level.

Pruning broad-leaved evergreens

Pruning is only necessary where frost damage has occurred. The following plants will stand pruning:

holly (*Ilex*)
cherry laurel (*Prunus laurocerasus*)

The different pruning techniques

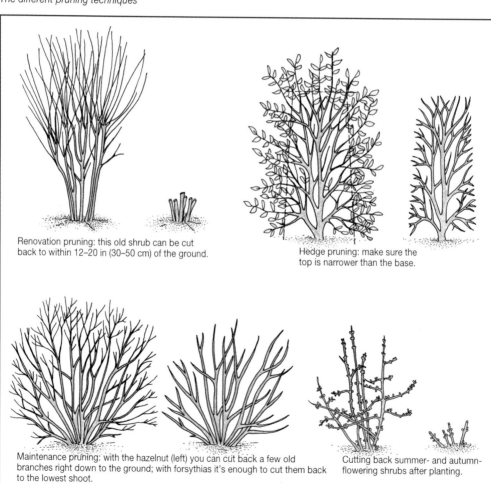

Renovation pruning: this old shrub can be cut back to within 12–20 in (30–50 cm) of the ground.

Hedge pruning: make sure the top is narrower than the base.

Maintenance pruning: with the hazelnut (left) you can cut back a few old branches right down to the ground; with forsythias it's enough to cut them back to the lowest shoot.

Cutting back summer- and autumn-flowering shrubs after planting.

Mahonia
box (*Buxus*)
ivy (*Hedera*)

and the evergreen forms of:
Cotoneaster
barberry (*Berberis*)
Euonymus
privet (*Ligustrum*)
Viburnum
ericaceous plants.

Many of these plants lose some of their leaves in spring, but this doesn't necessarily mean they've been damaged by frost. It's best to wait until June before deciding which parts need removing.

Renovation pruning

Sometimes a shrub needs radical renovation pruning, for instance when it has grown too big and hardly flowers any more, or looks really 'old'. Severe frost damage may also require this kind of treatment. February is the usual time for renovation pruning, though with spring-flowering plants you should wait until they've stopped flowering. The cure is a drastic one — cutting back the stems and branches to within about 12 in (30 cm) of the ground — but the plant will grow back again more effectively than if you cut back less dramatically. And if you apply some extra fertiliser, this will also help the plant to develop new shoots.

The following plants will tolerate renovation pruning:

barberry (*Berberis*)
beauty berry (*Callicarpa*)
Caryopteris

This ornamental hazel (Corylus) should be left unpruned if possible.

Ceanothus (in sheltered gardens)
Deutzia
spindle tree (*Euonymus europaeus*)
Hibiscus
Mahonia
Weigela
Kerria
holly (*Ilex*).

Shrubs that should never be pruned

Some shrubs that should never be touched with a saw or secateurs. These include some of the particularly attractive flowering shrubs, and also many of those with ornamental foliage. In both cases regular pruning should be avoided, though renovation pruning may occasionally be necessary. The time for that is in late winter, when the flower buds are visible and can therefore be protected.

Pruning conifers

In general conifers don't tolerate pruning as well as deciduous trees. With many of them this is because they grow symmetrically and the growth habit will be spoiled by pruning. This is especially true of firs (*Abies*), spruces (*Ficea*), true cedars (*Cedrus*), false cypresses (*Chamaecyparis*) except when grown as hedges, and all columnar species and varieties.

On the other hand, the bushier forms of yew (*Taxus*) and juniper (*Juniperus*) pose no such problems. Mountain pines (*Pinus mugo*) can lose whole branches every two or three years without their growth or appearance being affected. With other pines you should only cut back the young shoots — although this is no problem with dwarf pines, because their young shoots can be cut down to less than half their length. This produces a bushier habit and makes them grow more slowly.

Regular pruning is also in order for all coniferous hedges, especially if you want to train them into artificial shapes such as balls, pyramids and animal figures.

Propagating shrubs

Vegetative propagation is normal for ornamental trees and shrubs. They can be propagated from hardwood, greenwood or root cuttings, or by means of layering or division.

Hardwood cuttings

Hardwood cuttings should be taken from the current year's shoots in mid- to late autumn, when they have ripened after the leaves have been shed. Cut them immediately below a bud,

as this will encourage rooting. Take cuttings about 12 in (30 cm) long and 0.2 in (0.5 cm) thick. Trim them horizontally across the top and diagonally across the bottom, and cut off the soft tip.

Dig out a narrow trench about 8 in (20 cm) deep in a sheltered border or nursery bed, with one vertical side and one sloping side. Put a thin layer of coarse sand into the base. Push the prepared cuttings into the sand

so that about three-quarters of each cutting is in the trench, leaning against the sloping side; space them 2 in (5 cm) apart. Fill in the trench with fine soil or potting compost. Your cuttings will root then or in the spring, and can be planted the following autumn.

The following plants can be propagated by means of hardwood cuttings: butterfly bush (*Buddleia davidii*), *Cotoneaster*, *Deutzia*, *Forsythia*, ivy

*Mezereon (*Daphne mezereum*) can be propagated by means of cuttings or layering.*

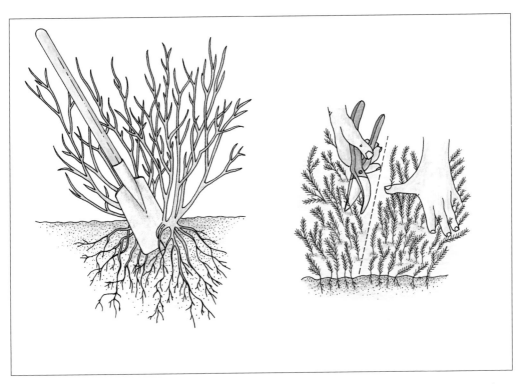

(*Hedera*), honeysuckle (*Lonicera*), *Parthenocissus*, *Philadelphus*, Russian vine (*Fallopia baldschuanica*), flowering currant (*Ribes sanguineum*), dogrose (*Rosa canina*), willow (*Salix*), elder (*Sambucus*), *Spiraea*, snowberry (*Symphoricarpos*), tamarisk (*Tamarix*), *Viburnum*, *Weigela*.

Semi-hardwood cuttings

You can take semi-hardwood cuttings in the summer. Make the cuttings between 2 in (5 cm) and 4 in (10 cm) long, and use shoots that have started to ripen at the base, so that the bark is brown but there is still a little greenness at the tip. Cut cleanly and directly below a leaf or pair of leaves, and remove the lower leaves on the stem, or they'll rot when the cutting is inserted.

Fill one or more 3-in (7.5-cm) or 3.5-in (9-cm) pots with compost up to within 0.5 in (1.5 cm) of the rim, and push in three or four cuttings around the side of each pot. Use a dibber or pencil to make a hole that'll be large enough to take one-half to two-thirds the length of each cutting, and make sure the base of the cutting is firmly on the bottom of the hole. Push the compost against the cutting so it won't move even when

*Heaths (*Erica*) can be divided using a pair of secateurs (right); for spiraeas you'll need a spade.*

gently pulled. If the leaves are large, cut them in half. Then put the pot (or pots) in a covered frame outdoors for the rest of the summer and autumn; don't let them dry out.

Taking cuttings from evergreens

The best time to propagate conifers and other evergreens is from late July to early August. Cuttings from conifers should be either torn off or removed with a small section of the old wood still attached. If you use a main

91

Layering is an effective method of propagating magnolia.

shoot, then cut it at the point where the current year's growth began. All spruces or firs should be propagated from a main shoot.

The cuttings should be 1-2 in (2-4 cm) long in the case of dwarf conifers, and 6-8 in (15-20 cm) long in the case of false cypress (*Chamaecyparis*), arbor-vitae (*Thuja*) or juniper (*Juniperus*). These three genera can be propagated quickly and easily, whereas other conifers need up to two years to take root. This applies, for example, to cedars, ginkgo, swamp cypress (*Taxodium*) or ornamental fir.

In the summer you should put your cuttings in a covered frame to protect them from direct sunlight and from excessive moisture.

Root cuttings

Plants that can be propagated from root cuttings include the stag's horn sumach (*Rhus hirta*), trumpet vine (*Campsis radicans*) and *Sorbaria tomentosa angustifolia*. Dig up the roots in the late winter, and cut them into pieces 3-4 in (8-10 cm) long, making sure the crown end of each root remains uppermost. Cut it straight across, and cut the base diagonally. Place the roots diagonally in pots or prepared beds, covering them with about 0.5 in (1 cm) of soil.

Simple layering

You can propagate many very beautiful shrubs and trees by simple layering. True, you'll only get a few specimens from a single parent plant, but the success rate is extremely high. Suitable candidates include: serviceberry (*Amelanchier laevis*), birch (*Betula*), Carolina allspice (*Calycanthus floridus*), hazel (*Corylus*), *Cotoneaster*, mezereon (*Daphne mezereum*), *Enkianthus campanulatus*, *Forsythia*, *Fothergilla gardenii*, witch hazel (*Hamamelis*), *Hydrangea*, honeysuckle (*Lonicera*), flowering currant (*Ribes*), lace shrub (*Stephanandra incisa*), *Symphoricarpos*, lilac (*Syringa*), *Viburnum*, *Wisteria* and a few rarer garden shrubs.

The best time for layering is in June or July. Take the flexible shoots that have grown during the early part of the year, bend them down to the ground, and use a wire peg to secure them in a small depression in the soil. Place a shallow layer of sand and compost over the spot, making sure the tip of the shoot is left visible. New roots will develop on the buried part of the shoot. The process will be quicker and more effective if you make a partial diagonal slit in this section below a leaf joint.

Rooting time varies considerably. Many new plants can be dug up and separated from the parent plant as early as the autumn, and then replanted in a sheltered location. Others won't develop into independent plants until the following spring. Never dig the plantlets up too soon. Some shrubs are often reluctant to root, in which case the best method is to lay the shoots in a pot filled with humus-rich soil.

Serpentine layering

Simple layering provides only one new plant from each shoot, because it's only the shoot tip that emerges from the soil. However, with some plants you can fix a long, thin shoot along the ground and cover it with soil, leaving just the buds exposed. A new plant will develop from each bud.

Division

Some shrubs push out suckers into the surrounding soil, which then take root and produce new plantlets of their own. Such plants can be propagated quite easily by division. Examples include Jew's mallow (*Kerria japonica*), stag's horn sumach (*Rhus hirta*), sea buckthorn (*Hippophae rhamnoides*), *Spiraea*, snowberry (*Symphoricarpos*) and *Viburnum*. Once the plantlets are sufficiently developed, they can be separated from the parent plant using a spade, dug up and replanted wherever you want. As the roots are not very extensive at this stage, it's best to remove the top section of each plantlet.

Plants that grow into thick clumps (e.g. *Erica*, *Deutzia*, *Spiraea*, *Mahonia*) can also be propagated by division. For this you will need to dig up the whole plant and carefully divide it into sections with a spade, or a pair of shears or secateurs. To be viable, each section must include at least one shoot with roots attached. It can then be replanted in a pot or a well-prepared bed. Again, remove the top growth of the new plantlet.

Hydrangeas can be propagated simply by layering, no matter what the species or variety.

93

Preventing pests and diseases

Pests and diseases are often a sign that a plant has been wrongly planted or poorly maintained — although bad weather conditions can also lead to fungal or insect infestations. No matter how careful you are about choosing the right plant for the right position, and providing the right amounts of water and nutrients, you will sometimes be faced with pests and diseases. However, there are ways of dealing with them.

Pests

Aphids

Shrubs may be infested with a whole variety of aphids in many different colours and sizes. If so, the leaves, buds and young shoots will show signs of damage such as curling and discoloration (mostly yellowing), while the leaves will become sticky with honeydew.

Cover low-growing shrubs with insecticidal powder containing pyrethrum or roterone (derris powder), and squirt with water to remove the pests. Treat serious infestations with repeated applications until they are controlled.

Scale insects

These pests settle on the undersides of leaves and the bark of stems, protected by distinctive round or oval scale-like shells, which are usually brown in colour. Young insects move about in late spring and early summer, and this is the best time for controlling them with a spray of bioresmethrin or malathion. Otherwise spray with tar oil in the winter, when the plants are dormant, to kill the adult scales and eggs.

Green spruce aphid

A dirty green insect with bright red eyes that leaves yellowish marks on the needles. After June the needles turn completely yellow, especially on older shoots, and fall prematurely. This pest most often affects the white spruce, and more rarely the Norway or Serbian spruce.

It can be combated with malathion, or by spraying with a soap solution in spring (or whenever you see it). You should also encourage aphid-eating insects such as earwigs, hoverfly maggots, ladybirds and their larvae.

Fruit-tree red spider mite

These tiny creatures infest the leaf undersides, where they suck the sap so that the leaves become speckled yellow and wither. In bad infestations they produce spider-like webbing, and the leaves wilt and eventually drop. Shrubs that are trained against walls are particularly susceptible.

Control is difficult. Hot, dry, sunny conditions encourage the appearance and spread of the mites, so make sure your plants always have adequate moisture at their roots. In hot weather, spray the top growth heavily with water several times a day, as well as watering the roots thoroughly.

Try malathion on infested plants, using about three applications at two-week intervals. However, many red spider mite populations are resistant. There will be some natural control if you don't use insecticides.

Vine weevils

This much-feared pest betrays its presence from June onwards, when U-shaped notches appear in the leaves of rhododendron, clematis and camellia. The only way to get rid of these insects is by picking them off bodily in May or June. As they only appear at night, you'll need a torch to find them.

The tiny white, brown-headed larvae, which feed on the roots, can be very effectively dealt with by introducing parasitic nematodes: they're available in proprietary products like Nemasys and Biosafe. Just put the nematodes in a watery solution and pour it over the area around the roots. This treatment is only effective between May and September, when the temperature is above 55°F (13°C) and the larvae are actually present; the soil should be thoroughly moist. Another method is to expose the roots and water them with a tansy infusion.

Caterpillars

Shrubs sometimes become infested with caterpillars like those of the winter moth, the ghost moth and the vine tortrix moth.

These can be treated with a caterpillar preparation such as Dipel. This contains a bacterium (*Bacillus thuringiensis*) that kills caterpillars but is harmless to bees and other beneficial insects. Spray the plant as soon as you see any caterpillars, or any signs of caterpillar damage.

Diseases

Mildew

Roses are particularly vulnerable to mildew. The stems, buds and leaves become covered with a powdery white coating, and infected flowers become dis-coloured. The shoots and buds then dry out and the leaves drop.

You can combat the problem by cutting out all affected shoots as soon as you see them, often as early as May. In June you should spray the plant with benomyl, or one of the propri-etary rose pesticides that con-tains fungicides to control black spot and rust as well. Remove all fallen leaves and destroy them, and water the plants in dry weather; in the autumn, cut out any infested growth that is present.

Stem rust in pines

Vulnerable plants include Weymouth pine (*Pinus strobus*), Arolla pine (*P. cembra*) and other pines with their needles grouped in fives. Swellings appear on the trunk and branches. These later burst open, releasing a yellow powder.

There is no cure. Affected plants are usually beyond saving, though you can some-times stop the rust spreading further by removing a single infected branch at once. Never plant blackcurrants close to pines, since they act as an alternative host during one stage in the rust's life cycle.

Needle drop in conifers

In August, older needles become discoloured and drop

There is no cure for stem rust in pines, and the plant is usually beyond saving.

off. This mostly happens around the inside of the tree, and is in fact a natural process. All needles have a limited lifespan, although its length varies in different species. Needle drop is severest in pines. Many plants become rather bare as a result, but soon recover the following year. Arbor-vitae and false cypress even form new shoots within the same year. It has been calculated that on average, conifers replace all their needles within a 3–5-year period.

If needle drop is unusually severe, this may be the result of heavy rain or drought, or of some pest or fungal infestation. Fungal infections will produce reddish or black spores on the underside of the needles; in some cases the needles will remain on the plant.

The only treatment for needle drop is to collect the fallen needles. If the trouble is due to a pest or disease, throw the needles away.

Index